..s of Old

Pl ˥, Bath and Avon

Tales of
Old Bristol
Bath and Avon

Jeannie Shorey

With Illustrations by Don Osmond

COUNTRYSIDE BOOKS
NEWBURY, BERKSHIRE

First Published 1989
© Jeannie Shorey 1989

COUNTRYSIDE BOOKS
3 CATHERINE ROAD
NEWBURY, BERKSHIRE

ISBN 1 85306 041 0

Produced through MRM Associates, Reading
Typeset by Acorn Bookwork, Salisbury
Printed in Great Britain by J W Arrowsmith Ltd., Bristol

To my late father Dennis Shorey
a real westcountryman

Contents

The plan overleaf is by Jacobus Millerd and shows Bristol as it was in the seventeenth century.

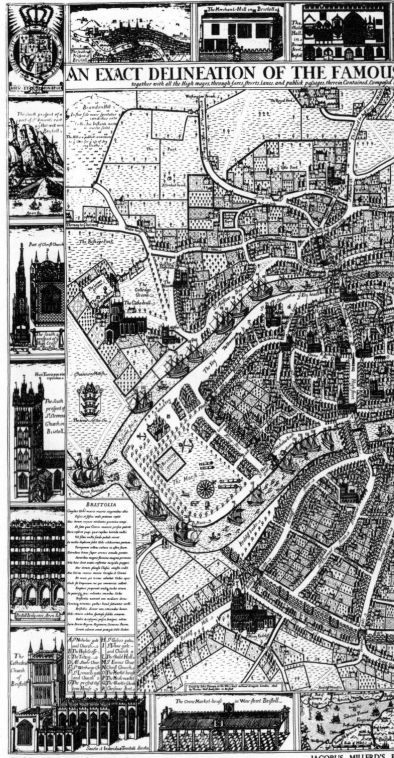

The Merchant-Hall in Bristoll

The Guild-Hall in a Bristoll

The South Prospect of Bristoll

AN EXACT DELINEATION OF THE FAMOUS

together with all the High-wayes, through-fares, streets, lanes, and publick passages, therein Contained, Composed

The South prospect of a part of St Vincents rock that well neere Bristoll

Avon flu.

Part of Christ Church

The south prospect of that Crosse in Bristoll

Hanc Turris pars vix sub... respicitur.

The South prospect of St Steevens Church in Bristoll

Bristoll Bridg over Avon flu...

The Cathedrall Church of Bristoll

Brandon Hill

The Park

The Bishops Park

The Greene

The Colledge Greene

The Cathedrall

Channons Marsh

The Key

The Marsh

BRISTOLIA

Coughut Urbi mari nigentibus altis
Fossa à fossa undè protena replet
...

A. St Nicholas gate and Church.
B. The High Crosse
C. The Tolzey
D. All Saints Chur.
E. St Werburgs Chu.
F. St Leonards gate and Church
G. The present Cuf tom House.
H. St Giles gate and Church
I. St Iohns gate and Church
L. The Guild Hall.
M. St Ewins Chur.
N. Christ Church.
O. The Market house
P. The Meale market
Q. The Gaunts church
R. Christmas street

The Corne Market-house in Wine-street Bristoll.

Sanctæ et Individuæ Trinitati dicata.

Original given to City Museum, Bristol, by Mr. Horace Gummer, 1923.

JACOBUS MILLERD'S P

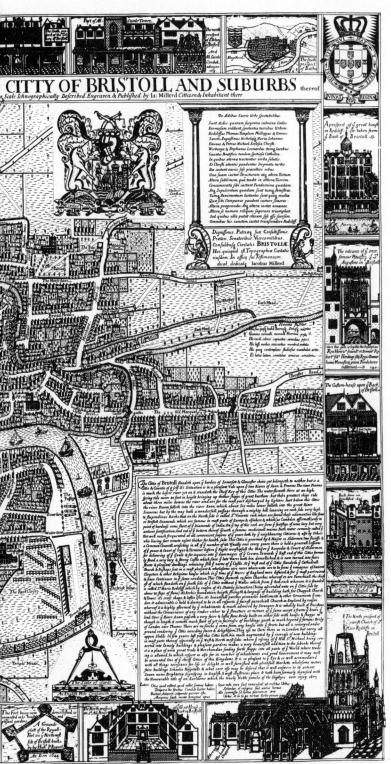

Printed by the City of Bristol Printing and Stationery Department 1979

Cold Duck Surprise

IN past centuries the retribution for 'lesser' crimes was often the use of stocks, pillories or ducking stools. These latter devices were a common punishment for immoral, nagging or scolding women and it was not uncommon for the culprit to drown due to an over-enthusiastic operator.

There was a ducking stool in Bristol which seems to have been in constant use from the 16th century until the punishment fell into disrepute. Somewhere under the old castle walls a post was set up in the water of the river Frome and across this post was a transverse beam turning on a swivel with a chair on the end. Culprits were placed in this chair, then they were turned to the murky waters and let down once, twice, or if particularly unlucky, three times. The last reported use of the Bristol ducking stool was in 1718 when the then Mayor of the city sentenced a particularly obnoxious woman for scolding her husband. On this occasion the Mayor lived to regret his action, for not only did he become the laughing stock of the city but also a lot poorer.

When Edmund Mountjoy was elected Mayor of Bristol it was known that, although he was a good man with a strong sense of civic responsibility, he was hen-pecked by a domineering wife. It was said of him that 'While he ruled the city, Mistress Mountjoy ruled him'! But there was not much he could do about it; he couldn't commit his wife to the ducking stool without appearing a fool himself.

One evening, when his wife was in a particularly quarrelsome mood, rather than tolerate her vicious tongue Mountjoy put on his hat and coat and decided to go into town. He felt very despondent and as people acknowledged him by taking off their hats as he passed he reflected that although he was treated with honour and dignity in the streets of Bristol he received no respect whatsoever at home. He was in this rather black mood when he passed a shop in the Hotwells area and a shrill voice caught his ear.

'You good-for-nothing, faint-hearted wretch,' it screamed, and at this the door opened and a huge woman pushed her meek-looking husband out into the street. 'You go and cool your legs in the air until you learn to return more quickly when I send you on an errand.' And with that she slammed the door.

Mountjoy paused for a moment, feeling sorry for the unhappy man. Then suddenly he saw an excellent opportunity for punishing in another his own wife's weakness. He would teach Mistress Mountjoy a lesson or at least show his power and perhaps gain a little of her respect. 'Officer,' he shouted to one who just happened to be passing, 'Officer, have that woman arrested. I will teach her that a man is master in his own house.'

Now the officer, of course, knew that his Worship the Mayor did not rule the roost at home and could hardly hold back a snigger, but with due deference he acted on orders and in time Mistress Blake, for that was her name, duly appeared before Chief Magistrate Mountjoy.

In court she kept up her tirade by giving the Mayor a 'piece of her mind'. 'Who does this man think he is for him to talk of a man being master in his own house when he dare not even sneeze inside his own without asking permission of his wife!' she roared.

The officers had great difficulty keeping control in the court, as spontaneous laughter burst out all around. 'Order, order,' cried Mountjoy, 'somebody silence that woman – if you can.' His Worship was now in such a rage that he pronounced the severest sentence for her 'crime'. 'To the ducking stool with her. Give her three dips and see if that doesn't cool her body and quench her tongue.'

When Mistress Blake went to the ducking stool in 1718 it was the last time that the people of Bristol would have the opportunity of witnessing the device at work. A vast crowd assembled. It was the scandal of the year and everyone wanted to see the Mayor's show of strength against the scolding spitfire. But the woman proved equal to the occasion. She never cried or called out and calmly submitted herself to her cold baths in the stinking, fetid water of the river Frome. Throughout the punishment the jovial crowd cracked the usual jokes about 'cold duck' and 'soused tongue'. Mistress Blake appeared oblivious to the taunts but as she was being unstrapped from the chair declared that she would have the last laugh at the expense of that 'hen-pecked craven man, Mountjoy, who only had the stomach to duck another man's wife.'

Mistress Blake proved as good as her word. As the time came for the end of Edmund Mountjoy's term of office, she forced her husband to bring about an action of battery on behalf of his wife and to enter a suit for damages against his ex-Worship the Mayor. So the scandal continued and the gossips had a field day. The Blakes employed a particularly strong prosecutor called Sir Peter King and after the trial at the Guildhall, the jury awarded such high damages to the defendant that no other Chief Magistrate ever dared to put the ducking stool into active use again. Thus it was that the institution fell into decay.

After some time had elapsed one enterprising Bristolian bought the old stool and turned the wood into snuff boxes. It was said that a pinch of snuff from one of these boxes possessed a charm which would protect a man from a scolding, domineering wife forever after!

From Bristol to
The New World

THE CITY OF BRISTOL can claim the title 'Birthplace of America', for although Christopher Columbus discovered a number of islands in the West Indies, it was a sailor from Bristol, John Cabot, who first landed on the mainland of America, in 1497. Bristolians also like to believe that the name 'America' comes from the Bristol merchant, Richard Ameryke, who was a friend and patron of Cabot and who helped finance the early journeys to that continent.

In the 15th century the Renaissance in Europe brought with it a great thirst for knowledge. People knew of the existence of India, China (Cathay) and even Japan and trading connections in those areas were well established. It was with those long eastern voyages that the concept of a round world had become plausible and it was not long before sailing west across the Atlantic to the 'Indies' was seriously being discussed in the courts of Europe. What the early explorers had not bargained for however was that the earth was much bigger than anyone had imagined and that a huge unknown continent lay between Europe and Asia.

John Cabot was born in Italy and had lived for a time

in Venice among other places. This ambitious man was an experienced mariner and had captained many voyages around the Mediterranean and beyond. Ships were conveyors of news as well as goods in those days so Cabot would have known about the voyage of his fellow-countryman Columbus and may even have met him when they were both in Valencia in 1493. Columbus had succeeded in gaining the confidence of the King and Queen of Spain who were persuaded to finance him, so if Cabot wanted to join in the race to the Orient he would have to look elsewhere and it was England with its great seafaring tradition that appeared to be the most promising prospect.

The English city which had the best experience in navigation at that time was Bristol, from whose port ships traded with all parts of the known world. It also had a good reputation for ship-building. So it was to Bristol that Cabot, with his wife Mattea and his three sons, came in 1495. He is known to have bought a house in the Saint Nicholas district and as soon as the family had settled set about his great task of funding an expedition to sail west to the Orient. It would probably have been at this time that he met Richard Ameryke who befriended and helped to finance him. Ameryke would have been well aware of the mercantile advantages to be gained from reaching the Orient directly from Bristol. To make the expedition official, however, Cabot needed royal patronage.

The Tudor King Henry VII had visited Bristol a few years previously and expressed an interest in finding a new route to the Indies. When he heard that there was an experienced captain preparing to launch an expedition in Bristol, he invited John Cabot to London to discuss the project. Cabot successfully gained the royal backing, for King Henry granted Letters Patent to him:

> 'To find isles, countries, regions or provinces of heathens and infidels whatsoever they be and in whatever part of the world soever they be which before this time have been unknown to all Christians and to set up our banners and ensigns and subdue, occupy and possess all such in the King's name.'

These were very full powers for anyone to have. The phrase 'unknown to all Christians' was important because he did not want to tread on Spanish toes. Cabot planned to go to a much higher latitude, far to the north of the Spanish interests.

And so it was that on 20th May 1497 John Cabot, with his crew of Bristolians, set off in the 70 ton caravel *Matthew*. Sailing across the great western sea into the unknown took a great deal of skill and courage. Navigation was still rather primitive. Sailors knew about latitude but had no means of measuring longitude, so at first Cabot steered to the most westerly point of Europe, near Bantry Bay in Ireland. From that point the *Matthew* sailed due west keeping as close to the same latitude as the winds would allow.

It must have been an anxious time for the crew of that little ship, waking up each morning to a vast, seemingly endless sea. But luck was with them. On 24th June, Midsummer Day, they sighted land, anchored and set foot on the mainland of North America. Records of the trip are very sparse so it is not known exactly where the first landing took place. The spot where Cabot first raised the flag could have been Newfoundland, Cap Breton or even Nova Scotia.

After the initial landfall the expedition followed the coast in a southerly direction, no doubt still hoping to discover Cathay. They did not find any form of civilisation and saw only vast forests and grasslands. The sea through which they sailed, which we now call the Grand Banks, was literally teeming with fish. Cabot and his crew must have realised that the area had great potential for agriculture, forestry and fishing. The *Matthew* sailed for about 800 miles down the coast and then Cabot decided to return to their original latitude to make sure of success on the homeward journey. With the wind in their favour that return crossing was made in 15 days and the expedition arrived back in Bristol on 6th August.

Cabot was received like a hero and was named the 'Grand Admiral'. After reporting his finds to his Bristol backers, including Ameryke, he set off for London to see the King. Henry was delighted with the discovery. He presented him with £10 immediately from the Privy Purse and granted him a pension of £20 a year. Almost overnight John Cabot became rich and famous. He was able to dress in the finest clothes and people followed him wherever he went, eager for knowledge of the new lands. The King gave his blessing for a second expedition the following year, authorising Cabot to take six English ships with him.

So Cabot spent the winter preparing his ships and crew, for this was to be a far bigger venture. Once more he appealed to Ameryke and the Bristol merchants for their help. From what he had discovered already, the potential trade in fishing and lumber made it well worth their while investing in the new expedition. Now as

Cabot was an Italian and probably had a strong foreign accent, it is quite conceivable that the people of Bristol preferred to refer to it as 'Ameryke's expedition' and this may well have been the origin of the name of the destination.

Five ships were eventually fitted out and among the travellers this time were a group of 'free emigrants', probably people from the Bristol area who volunteered to stay behind, farm the land and set up the first colony. Everything they needed to survive had to go with them, and there were two priests to cater for their religious needs and to convert the heathen natives. Also aboard were some experienced diplomats, for at that stage it was still not certain that the land was not in fact part of Asia; Cathay might have been just around the corner!

Cabot's second expedition left Bristol in the summer of 1498. Within weeks of the departure two of the five ships had returned due to storm damage in mid-Atlantic. After that – silence. Nothing was ever heard of John Cabot or his expedition again. They simply disappeared in the vastness of the New World! There are many things that could have happened to them – shipwreck, famine or disease, or they could have been killed by hostile natives. One of the more popular theories is that Cabot sailed so far south that he reached the Gulf of Mexico in the hurricane season. We shall never know.

But John Cabot had helped to open the door to this new land and in time many others were to follow him. People began to realise that the new land was not Cathay, nor indeed any part of Asia, but a huge new continent ripe for development.

Portishead Wreckers and Pill Sharks

'The tide runs up, the tide runs down;
'Tis forty-five feet at Possett Town
The tide do ebb and the tide do flow
And the deadly sand it do lie below.
The deadly sand it do crawl around,
And there's many a tall ship cast aground,
And there's many a craft in sight of land
That is swallowed up by the deadly sand.
Down a down, down a down
The deadly sand do drag them down.'

THE BRISTOL CHANNEL, with its treacherous shifting quicksands and huge tides which rise as high as 45 feet in places, is a dangerous water through which to navigate. In the days when the great sailing ships used to return from their long voyages heavily laden with tobacco, sugar, silks and spices, skilled pilots were needed to guide them through the perilous waters into the port of Bristol.

Only the local pilots knew the safe routes to the mouth of the Avon and the villages of Portishead and Pill produced the best. In the busy King Road anchorage just off Avonmouth, sailing ships would wait for a high tide and a suitable wind to carry them down the Channel and out into the Atlantic Ocean. The pilots' boats would mingle among them and when a merchant ship was spotted heading in they would race each other down the Channel. Whoever was the fastest got the job. At high tide pilots would guide the great ships as far as Pill, where the crew would be 'paid off' and the ship would continue the journey up the Avon to the port of Bristol, either rowed by special tugboats or towed by a team of horses on the riverside tow path.

There was great rivalry between the pilots of Portishead and Pill and it was not always friendly. The Portishead men were known as the 'Wreckers' and they had no reason to feel piqued at their nickname. In the past many had been guilty of wrecking and looting and on one occasion they were even known to have been helped by the local clergy.

Portishead stands on a rocky outcrop just before the land flattens out at the mouth of the river Avon. The practice of the wreckers was to light fires on the shore between the rocky headlands or to 'black out' one of the official lights in order to confuse an unwitting ship into coming in too close to the shore. They would wait callously for a ship to sink, then swoop on the wreckage and its survivors. As it was against the law to take salvage if anyone from a wrecked ship was still alive, that law virtually condemned any survivors to death. On rare occasions the wreckers reaped a rich harvest and the whole town was involved in sharing the spoils, but because of the nature of the Portishead coastline most attempts failed. Many a time an unsuspecting ship would falter and sink in the deadly off-shore quicksands and both crew and cargo would be lost.

When being taunted by their rivals as 'wreckers', the Portishead men would reply derisively by calling the Pill men 'sharks'. The latter had acquired this name many years before after a particular incident during a time when there was a great shortage of food in the Severnside area.

One day the pilots received news that two merchant ships were due in from the West Indies and the rival boats raced down the Channel as far as the Isle of Lundy to see who could win the prize. The Pill pilot reached the larger vessel first but, to the amazement of the Portis-head team, seemed to falter and dropped behind the ship thus allowing them to claim the piloting fee. The Pill boat then seemed to disappear behind the smaller ship too, before eventually taking it in tow.

After a hard journey up the Bristol Channel, the Portishead men were pleased with themselves as they brought the West Indiaman safely into Pill where horse teams were ready to tow it to the Bristol quays. They stayed behind for a while to mock the Pill pilots when they arrived for their clumsiness at sea in losing the bigger prize. Still laughing, the men returned to Portis-head, but although they had been well paid they still had to face empty larders when they got home.

The next day when the women of Portishead met the women from Pill it was they who were the object of derision. The wives of Pill took much delight in telling them that the previous night the whole town had been feasting on roast pork and plenty of it! 'Couldn't you smell it up in Portishead, then?' they jeered.

The citizens of Pill had indeed dined on pork, a little salty perhaps but none the worse for that. It was from the pig carcasses which had been towed behind both the merchant ships as shark bait while they were far out at sea. The captains had forgotten about them but the wily Pill pilots had collected the meat from both ships, a 'prize' which they regarded as far more important than the larger piloting fee!

When the wives returned to Portishead and told their husbands the story they were furious and from that day called their rivals 'Sharks'.

A Dream
of an
Invention

ONE night in the year 1782 a Bristol man woke up suddenly and jumped out of bed in a state of great agitation. Had he been a more educated person he would probably have shouted 'Eureka!'. But William Watts was an ordinary plumber by trade who lived with his wife in a modest house on Redcliffe Hill. Because of his vocation he was used to working with lead and had for many years been pondering on the question of how to make perfect lead shot. Now he thought he had the answer.

The cause of Watts' excitement was a dream; a dream in which he visualised raindrops or a waterfall or ... whatever it was, it gave him the idea for a totally new method of making shot.

In the late 18th century there was a great demand for good shot both for military purposes and for sporting guns, a demand which far outstripped supply. The production process was very slow and tedious and the resulting ammunition was both expensive and unreliable.

Even though it was the middle of the night Watts was eager to try out his idea while it was still fresh in his mind. His wife, who had been wakened by his initial excitement, was only too pleased to help; she was willing to co-operate with anything that might make them a fortune! William first of all placed a bowl of cold water at the foot of the stairwell and then started to heat up some lead at the top of the stairs. After what must have seemed like an age, the metal was fully molten and Mrs Watts held up a kitchen colander through which William poured the liquid metal very carefully, allowing it to fall the height of the stairwell into the cold water below. The result was perfectly formed, spherical lead shot.

After examining the cold shot they repeated the experiment several more times just to make sure that it wasn't a fluke. The couple were delighted with their work – and it was so simple. It meant no more plumbing jobs for William, for with this easy method of shot manufacture the hoped-for fortune was virtually guaranteed. Sure enough later that year he was granted Letters Patent for his new process. Thus it was that the enterprising plumber of Redcliffe Hill turned his house into a small manufactory of lead shot.

When the word spread many others tried to copy Watts' method of production and without exception they all failed. It was incredible. 'How did the Bristol man succeed?' they asked themselves. Unknown to him at the time William Watts' experiment did have an element of luck attached. The reason for his success was that there was an extra ingredient in his source of metal, which he obtained from some old Roman lead workings high in the Mendips. Later, when analysed, the impurity turned out to be arsenic! The presence of arsenic in the lead he used changed the physical properties of the metal allowing spheres to form on solidification. Using normal lead the metal formed long strings instead.

William Watts' dream discovery proved to be a winner and his business rapidly prospered. After a time many of his customers began to ask if he could make them smaller shot. Now this posed another problem. He thought long and hard about it and came to the conclusion that the way to do it might be to increase the height of the fall.

Undaunted, he cut a hole in the roof and to the astonishment of his neighbours built a tower on top of his house. Cautiously he experimented, pouring the metal from the higher level. It worked. The new smaller-sized shot sold equally well and the money continued to pour in.

But within another couple of years the development of more sophisticated weapons led the customers to demand even smaller-sized ammunition. There was only one way to increase the height of the drop still further – beneath the tower and the stairwell, William Watts dug down under his house to create a deep well!

In the end the house on Redcliffe Hill could stretch no further, so in 1792, ten years after his initial dream, William Watts sold his invention to a local ammunition company, who constructed a specially high shot tower for the process. Mr and Mrs Watts collected £100,000 from the sale of the patent, a vast fortune in those times which enabled the plumber and his wife to live in comfort for the rest of their lives.

The
Charfield
Rail Disaster

ONE of the great mysteries of Avon concerns a terrible
rail disaster which occurred on 13th October 1928.
In one corner of the churchyard at Churchend near
Charfield is the large common grave of the victims of that
disaster and over it there stands an impressive monument erected by the London, Midland and Scottish
Railway Company displaying the names of the dead. At
the end of that list, separated from the others are the
words – 'Two Unknown'. What makes the mystery even
more poignant is that the unknown bodies were those of
small children.

That chilly autumn morning in October 1928 was
foggy and visibility was down to only 30 yards. At
Charfield station a goods train was just leaving the main
line for a siding in order to clear the line when, without
warning, the Newcastle to Bristol passenger express
crashed into it at full speed. To add to the destruction,
another goods train coming up from Bristol on the
northbound track collided with the wreckage in the thick
fog. It was total chaos. Carriages were piled up, under

and against the bridge near the station. Local people later remembered hearing an explosion and noticing a red glow through the murky morning light. Gas cylinders, used in those days for lighting trains, had blown up on impact and so strong was the blast that one man was thrown on to the roadway of the bridge above; he had been shot clean through the roof of his compartment. Fire broke out everywhere and flames trapped passengers beneath the twisted mass of debris. Some of the bodies were charred beyond recognition.

To make matters even worse, the rescue services took much longer than usual to reach the scene of the accident because of the poor visibility on the country roads that morning. In the end the official human toll was 15 killed and 23 badly injured. It was the worst rail disaster the area had ever known.

Identifying some of the remains proved a difficult and grisly task. Bodies were recognised by such personal effects as buttons, tie pins and cigarette cases. In one case a wife recognised some clothing which had been recovered from the wreckage because she herself had mended it for her husband. But there was nothing by which the bodies of the children could be identified.

One by one a sad procession of relatives and friends from all over the country came forward to claim the crash victims and gradually all were spoken for; all that is except the two small bodies of the children. As time passed the police became more and more anxious to establish their identity. Careful checking revealed that no children had been reported missing in the country. One man reported that he thought he saw two children in school uniform board the train at Gloucester but this line of enquiry came to nothing, for the man could not remember whether the youngsters were accompanied or even the colour of their uniform, only that they were a boy and a girl. Exhaustive enquiries by police and railway officials failed to bring to light any clue about them.

When all investigations and forensic probing had failed, the little bodies were interred in the mass grave and their only record of existence remains as – 'Two Unknown'. It seems strange that no one enquired about them either at the time or since. The mystery remains unsolved today over 60 years on.

The
Uncrowned
King of Bath

THE visit of Queen Anne to Bath in 1702 was regarded by the city as an occasion for great celebration. A new road was specially constructed for her to
travel into the city from Lansdown and on arrival she
was welcomed by 100 young men dressed as warriors
and 200 young women dressed as Amazons. An
ornamental triumphal arch was erected in her honour
and so many people came to see the Queen that the city
was crowded to capacity, despite the fact that the cost of
lodgings soared to one guinea a night! Had they but
known, it was to be the start of a new era for Bath, one
which would transform it from an obscure watering
place into the most fashionable spa in Europe, and the
man who was to create this phenomenon just happened
to arrive in Bath on the same day as Queen Anne.

Richard Nash, born in 1674, was in no way a handsome man, being described as having a red, heavy face
with watery blue eyes and a clumsy figure. He did have
the benefit of a good education and went to Jesus College, Oxford in 1692. However, he seems to have wasted

his time there and left rather abruptly after a scandalous affair with a young woman. In fact he left in such a hurry that he owed money to his college and to this day that debt has still not been cleared. After this he spent a short time in the army and then became a law student, but neither of these professions appealed to him. The young man had developed a taste for elegant clothes, fine wine and extravagant living and to finance this costly lifestyle he eventually took up gambling as a career.

Queen Anne's royal visit to Bath brought in its wake a flood of people from the rich, fashionable classes whose main hobby at the time was gambling. So when Richard Nash first came to the city he did so with high hopes of replenishing his purse. With rooms at one guinea a night he needed to be successful to pay his way!

To organise the social events of the city Bath Corporation employed a Master of Ceremonies. At the time of Nash's arrival this position was held by a Captain Webster. Nash and Webster struck up a friendship and soon young Richard became the Captain's 'aide-de-camp'. He also proved very successful in his chosen career and was reputed to have been earning about £100 a week at the gaming tables. So his decision to come to Bath proved to have been a good one and with his winnings he could indulge in his expensive passions to the full. His clothes, made of silk and satin, were the best that money could buy and he always wore a white tricorned hat. He bought a grand house in St John's Court where he entertained lavishly. Such a pillar of society did he become that when Captain Webster was killed by a sword in a skirmish the Corporation immediately appointed Richard Nash as his successor.

The city was soon to benefit from Nash's 'reign'. He

33

outlawed the wearing of swords in public and brought down the cost of lodgings. The river Avon was made navigable and this enabled supplies and building materials to be shipped in from the port of Bristol. It was decreed that pavements were to be laid to serve the splendid new houses and Assembly Rooms which were being built. Each household was made responsible for lighting the streets and was obliged to hang out lanterns between 14th September and 25th March from dusk to midnight. The streets were cleared of beggars and loiterers and harsh penalties were meted out for petty crimes. Under Nash's rule even the sedan chair drivers had to toe the line and charge set rates.

Because of his elegant lifestyle and his 'trendsetter' image, Richard Nash was known affectionately as 'Beau' and as his popularity increased he drew up a set of 'Rules of Behaviour' for citizens and visitors which were displayed all over the town. These rules included – 'that ladies shall not be seen in the Assembly Rooms in aprons' and 'no gentleman should attend a dance wearing boots'. They were obeyed implicitly. It was a comedy of manners and the people loved it. More and more visitors came to the city to see and to be seen. Bath's Master of Ceremonies seemed to know exactly what his people wanted; he was an entrepreneur with a genius for organisation.

The day in fashionable 18th century Bath followed a set pattern. People rose early in order to take the waters and shortly afterwards bathing began. Both sexes 'bathed' at the same time; they just walked about in the water fully clothed. Ladies had little trays fixed to the waist which floated in front of them and on which were carried their necessities – a handkerchief, puff box and snuff. After a while the bathers were helped out of the water by their servants, wrapped in towels and taken home by sedan chair to dry out in front of their own fires. For the rest of the morning there were lectures, concerts or church services. On fine afternoons it was the custom to take a walk in the Parade or the Grove. Dinner was taken in the late afternoon and evenings were spent in the Assembly Rooms drinking tea, dancing or playing cards. Dances began at six o'clock and finished promptly at 11 pm. When 11 o'clock struck Beau Nash himself would give the signal to the band to stop and no-one, not even a Duchess, would dare ask for another dance.

Nash never married. He had several mistresses of whom the only lasting one was a dressmaker called Juliana Papjoy. She earned herself the title of 'Lady Betty Besom' because of her habit of riding round the streets on a dapple-grey horse carrying a many-thonged whip.

Beau Nash enjoyed a long and full life but towards the end his luck began to run out on the gaming tables. With the introduction of new games and his own creeping senility the Beau started to lose money. He sold his house and moved to a smaller one in Saw Close next to the theatre, where he was looked after in his old age by Juliana Papjoy. The once splendid wardrobe began to show signs of wear although he still insisted on wearing his famous white hat wherever he went and in the mornings always dressed in a gown of red and white satin, lined with white Persian lamb.

The uncrowned King of Bath died on 12th February 1761 at the age of 86. His body lay in state for four days and afterwards he was given a magnificent funeral by the Corporation and buried in Bath Abbey. As the funeral procession made its way to the Abbey on that unhappy day, crowds filled the streets to pay homage to their 'King'. Faces peered down from every window and even the tops of the houses were covered with spectators. The last time the streets had been so crowded was on that far-off day when Queen Anne visited Bath and a young man walked into the city to seek his fortune.

Angels of the Avon

IN the past the threat of plague and disease was a real and constant fear for people living in the overcrowded conditions of our cities. Water supplies and sanitary arrangements were primitive and outbreaks of plague were much more common than we care to think. Whereas the great plagues of the 14th and 17th centuries were national or international, many other outbreaks were confined to just one area, like that which struck Bristol in 1551 during the reign of Edward VI.

Around Easter time of that year two cases suddenly occurred in the Redcliffe district of the city and they were both fatal. News of the deaths spread quickly – so did the plague, but at first it was confined to the area south of the Avon. There was then only one bridge connecting the north and south of the city. This was Bristol Bridge, which was in the same position as the modern bridge of that name but very different in appearance. The old Bristol Bridge supported houses right across its span, rather akin to the old London Bridge or the Ponte Vecchio in Florence. The old Bristol Bridge actually had a chapel in its centre and, it was to this chapel in 1551 that worshippers who lived on or near the bridge thronged daily, praying to be spared from the danger and affliction which had befallen the city.

There used to be a popular belief that running water was a preventative against the passage of infectious disease so Bristolians who lived to the north of the river thought they would be quite safe so long as they kept the river between them and the infected south. Public opinion was so strong that it was decided to place a guard on Bristol Bridge to prevent people crossing the Avon in either direction.

In Redcliffe the pestilence continued to claim victims and now the unfortunate people had to contend not only with the terrible disease in their midst but also with the problems of isolation. They could not get any fresh vegetables or provisions either from the city or from the farmers and people of Somerset as nobody wanted to run the risk of entering the plague area. Thus they faced virtual starvation.

During the reign of Henry VIII a convent, dedicated to Saint Mary Magdalene, had stood on the site of the King David Inn on Saint Michael's Hill, but like many others it had been suppressed during the Reformation. The nuns were scattered; some had returned to their families, others had joined convents in France, but six of the younger sisters, all daughters of Bristol merchants, had stayed together in the city and lived in a quiet house with a walled garden in Baldwin Street. When news of the plague reached them they were as horrified as everyone else at first but after a few days of contemplation they decided to leave their house and go to the assistance of the afflicted people of Redcliffe. It was a brave step in many ways. Since they had taken the veil they had led very secluded lives; none of them had mixed with others or gone abroad into the world of men. Their bold idea came from a genuine desire to help their stricken neighbours.

The six sisters soon found out that there was no free passage across the bridge. Undaunted, they decided to hire a boat to cross the river and so transport vital provisions and medicine to the people of Redcliffe. In an old shed they established a depot for food and clothing and anything else charitably minded people might give them. Because no boatman would help them, they had to work the little boat themselves. They ferried it across the Avon back and forth, happy in the belief that the passage across the running water of the river purified them of infection. The good sisters kept up this service for many days, their kindness and concern being welcomed by the distressed people of Redcliffe. They carried food and water to the dying and their families, often walking through dark deserted streets where braziers of charcoal and pitch burned day and night to purify the infected air.

After a time the dreaded plague did spread to the rest of the city and continued to scourge Bristol until Michaelmas of that year, killing hundreds every week. The courageous group of sisters gave themselves entirely to their work. They even organised other women into bands of nurses, as well as continuing to distribute food and medicine on both sides of the river. But gradually the disease took its toll and they too succumbed. One by one they fell, until just before Michaelmas the last and bravest of the sisters started with the 'sweating sickness' and died within the day.

When the plague abated the angelic women and their

great sacrifice were not forgotten. The people of Redcliffe remembered them in their church. Until the end of the 19th century there was a stained glass window in the north transept of the church of Saint Mary Redcliffe which depicted them in their little boat ferrying themselves across the Avon on their heroic mission.

Terror
on the
Old Bath Road

IN the 18th century anyone who travelled to Bath by coach faced many dangers and discomforts. The roads were badly rutted, so that coaches often became stuck in the mud or overturned. Axles and wheels broke, horses became lame, luggage fell off and the jolting was so rough that occupants were sometimes thrown out. In the winter when conditions were at their worst a journey of 40 miles could take up to 14 hours and if this were not enough misery there was also the constant threat of highway robbery.

Highwaymen were common throughout England, as there was no police force and it was difficult to enforce the king's justice outside the towns. They were not at all like the glamourous character portrayed in the Noyes' poem –

'He'd a French cocked-hat on his forehead, a bunch of
    lace at his chin,
A coat of claret velvet and breeches of brown doeskin.'

With few exceptions they came from the dregs of society, hardened criminals often driven by poverty to this particular way of life.

The West Country roads leading to Bath were famous haunts for highwaymen. Gibbets were erected at main crossroads to deter them but had little effect, such were the rich pickings to be had from travellers bound for the gaming tables and Assembly Rooms.

A most notorious gang of highwaymen terrorised this area in the 1750s. They held up coaches in broad daylight, threatening the occupants with pistols and taking not only money but also jewellery, wedding rings, watches, clothes and anything else of value. The gang was led by a tough character called John Poulter who at one time had sworn an oath that he would never be captured alive. His very appearance was terrifying; a tall, swarthy man with a thick scar on his cheek. He made no attempt at disguise and had several times used his pistol on people who tried to defy him. Poulter led a gang of equally desperate men, outlaws and other fugitives from justice. There was no shortage of such men willing to join them, nor of the women followers who looked after them and always made sure there were plenty of stolen horses for a quick getaway. Poulter's operations were very successful and he is known to have travelled as far afield as Jamaica spending or trading his ill-gotten gains. When he had spent up he always returned to Bath to prey once more on the long-suffering travellers.

One afternoon in 1753 Poulter and his men held up and robbed a coach on Claverton Down just outside the city. From a Doctor Hancock he stole £35, a gold watch and some silver plate worth £150. There is no record of what he took from the other passengers but on that occasion one of them must have proved rather awkward, for Poulter suddenly grabbed a child from the coach and threatened to kill it if the man did not 'deliver'. This action incensed the travellers so much that, when they arrived in Bath, Doctor Hancock personally led a strong protest and demanded that action be taken to catch the villain. The Hue and Cry went out. The threat to kill an innocent child was strongly emotive and in response the local newspapers offered a huge reward for the capture of 'John Poulter, Highwayman'.

Somewhere in the hills around Bath the Poulter gang had a secret hide-out where they thought they were safe. Only members of the gang and their women knew of its whereabouts and it was well guarded. However, the temptation of that huge reward offered by the newspapers proved too strong. There was no 'honour among thieves' for John Poulter this time; he was betrayed by one of his own men. The informer bribed the look-outs and the gang was taken by surprise. They were overpowered and their leader was taken alive.

Highway robbery was an odious crime in the eyes of the law and the travelling public cried out for justice. They would settle for nothing less than execution. The verdict of 'guilty' was unanimous and the judge showed no mercy. John Poulter was hanged from the gibbet on Claverton Down, close to the scene of his last fateful robbery.

The
Avenging Bull
of
Chipping Sodbury

ॐ

QUEEN MARY TUDOR was probably the most un-
loved and unsuccessful of all English monarchs. She
spared no effort in her determination to restore Catholicism to her realm and the title 'Bloody Mary' was well-
earned. During her reign of only five years as many as
300 people were burnt at the stake as heretics. Four of
these were from Chipping Sodbury.

In those uneasy times the Catholic Church appointed
special officials known as vicar-generals who were responsible for keeping religious order and for exposing
and sentencing non-believers. The market town of Chipping Sodbury was unfortunate in having a particularly
bloodthirsty vicar-general called Doctor Whittington.
Almost as soon as he arrived in the area he made himself
unpopular in the town by condemning a highly-
respected citizen, named John Piggot, to be burnt at the
stake just because he would not stand up in church and
publicly renounce his Protestant beliefs. Some time later

two other men, John Barnard and John Walsh, were also sentenced to public execution by fire. Whittington had accused them of trying to incite the people against him. They had in fact been trying to draw public attention to the harsh punishment meted out by the authorities by showing Piggot's blackened bones to a small gathering.

Mary had hoped that as time went on the people would succumb to her wishes that they should revert to Catholicism. But she failed to understand that the common people associated it with foreign influence, particularly with the Spanish Inquisition. As a result more and more people were martyred.

In Chipping Sodbury Doctor Whittington needed another victim to placate his masters and he vindictively chose, as a scapegoat, a poor woman who had no family. He accused her of heresy and she was duly sentenced to death. The citizens were rightly angered but without putting themselves and their families in danger what could they do? The identity of the woman has been lost, but it is known that she was reputed to be a good, devout person.

On the day of the execution nearly everyone in the town turned out to see the poor woman bravely meet her fate and many a silent prayer was offered up for her as the fire was kindled. In a prominent position among the crowd was Doctor Whittington. Zealously believing that he was doing what was required of him, he stood merciless and unflinching as the flames leapt higher. The woman vehemently protested her innocence and even during her terrible suffering in the flames insisted that she was going to heaven with a clear conscience.

Now at the very time of the execution it so happened that in another part of the town the local butcher was about to slaughter a fine bull. There were no humane killing methods in those days; the animal was tied up while the butcher carefully chose his weapon. As the man raised the heavy axe to kill the bull it suddenly moved its head and the blow missed! Perhaps aware of its fate and certainly startled by the noise of the falling axe, the bull panicked, broke loose from its ropes and escaped into the main street of the town.

The street was packed with the sombre crowds returning from the execution, their minds, no doubt, still numb from the scene they had just witnessed. The sober mood was suddenly broken by the sight of a rampant bull charging towards them. Scattering in all directions to allow the frightened animal to pass through, miraculously no-one was hurt.

The bull galloped on towards the market square where Doctor Whittington and his officials were still standing over the charred remains of their victim. Seeing the Doctor's bright red cloak and maddened by the stench of burning it snorted, pricked up its ears and charged towards him at full speed.

Whittington had no chance. The angry bull gored him, killing him outright and his body was symbolically impaled on the sharp horns. A second execution had taken place that day in the market square of Chipping Sodbury and poetic justice had triumphed over human injustice.

The Swineherd Prince

WHEN the Romans discovered the naturally hot mineral springs in the lower Avon valley they immediately set about building a city around them. Thermal bathing appealed to them and to find spring water which was already heated was an added bonus, especially in the harsh climate of Britain. They built baths, temples, hostels and villas and soon people came from all over the northern Roman Empire to 'The Waters of Sul' – Aquae Sulis. Unlike other cities, which were usually built as military or administrative centres, Aquae Sulis, now known as Bath, was built primarily as a recreation and leisure centre.

However, the Romans were not the first to discover the special properties of the waters of Bath. Local tribes were already using the hot springs as a centre for magic and healing. These people worshipped the god Sul and believed it was he who mysteriously heated the water. Sacred springs were common in ancient Britain but this one was special. Many people travelled for days to reach the place; the sick, the maimed and the diseased, particu-

larly lepers, all waiting for a chance to immerse themselves in Sul's waters.

Some of them might have had reason to thank a certain
Prince Bladud. For it is said that long long ago, before
the rise of the Roman Empire, a powerful king called
Lud Hudibras ruled over the land of Britain. But tragedy
struck this great king, for his eldest son and heir, Prince
Bladud, darling of the royal court, was suddenly smitten
with leprosy. The shock was felt throughout the land.
This horrible disease was known to be contagious and
sufferers, whether they were princes or ploughmen, were
cast out of society. So King Hudibras had no choice but
to banish his son from the court and leave him to wander
the countryside and live as best as he could. Before
Bladud left the palace his mother, the Queen, gave him a
ring, a token to present to her on his return should he
ever recover, or at worst to buy himself some comfort in
his hours of torment.

The young prince travelled for many days, full of
bitterness at having to leave his rich and happy life for an
existence little better than a living death. At first he lived
on berries, wild fruit and food which kind-hearted
peasants left at the roadside for such as him. Finding
himself in the valley of the Avon, he had the good fortune
to meet a farmer who took pity on his plight and
promised him food and clothes in return for looking after
a herd of pigs. Bladud was delighted to do so; even
herding swine was better than being in constant danger
of starvation! In those days pigs were herded much as
sheep were in later times; swineherds allowed them to
wander for weeks at a time, grubbing up acorns and any
other food that they could find in the forests.

After the initial elation however, bad luck overtook

Bladud once more. To his horror he noticed that the pigs had contracted his dreadful disease. Terrified of his master finding out, he asked the farmer if he could drive the herd to the other side of the Avon, pretending that he believed there to be better acorns on the other side. Permission was granted. The shallow in the river where Bladud and his pigs crossed is still called Swineford.

Tired and full of anguish at this latest blow to his fortunes, Bladud wandered along the banks of the river to a place near some swampy ground with warm steam rising from it and here he spent the night. When he awoke next morning he found his pigs wallowing in the mud and steaming waters of the swamp, apparently loving every minute of it.

Casually observing his pigs the following day he noticed to his surprise that they were beginning to lose some of their leprous scabs. Curious, he washed some of the animals down and found that their skin had almost completely healed! If it was the swampy water which had cured the pigs, then would it not also be beneficial to a man in the same condition? He immersed himself in the muddy pool several times and to his delight found that his skin gradually became whole and clean once more. By the time they had left the swamp, prince and pigs were completely cured.

Losing no time he retraced his steps across the river and returned the herd to his master who must have been surprised to see the young man so fit and well. Then Bladud set off with gusto on his journey home. Arriving at the palace he presented his mother with the ring and the royal parents were overjoyed to have their beloved son miraculously restored to them once more.

Bladud eventually became King of Britain and one of

the first acts of his reign was to send men to the swamp in the Avon valley where he had found the healing waters. They cleaned the springs and built a town on the spot where others who were afflicted might also be cleansed. Word spread and people came hopefully to the healing waters of Sul, just as people still come to the healing waters of Bath, many hundreds of years later.

King John's
Castle

ON the red shield of the heraldic coat of arms of the city of Bristol a medieval ship is shown emerging from the battlements of a great castle and Bristol Castle, built in the 12th century by Robert, Earl of Gloucester, was indeed a great castle. Built of sandstone, it was twice the size of Caernarvon and had a keep larger than the Tower of London. The outer walls were 25 feet thick at the base and nine feet thick at the top and within those impregnable walls were living quarters, a chapel, stables, a parade ground and a grand banqueting hall.

When the future King of England, John, married Hawisia, daughter and heiress of the Earl of Gloucester, it was agreed in the marriage contract that he should inherit the estate on the Earl's death. So when the Earl died, John became Lord of Bristol. When he also became King of England he divorced Hawisia but kept the castle, estates and title.

Bristol Castle became one of the principal castles in England and during the earlier reign of John's brother Richard the Lionheart, who was frequently away on Crusades, Prince John had made it his headquarters from where he ruled the country in his brother's name.

After his divorce John married the 14 year old Isabelle of Angouleme. The fact that she was already betrothed to one of his Norman nobles did not bother him. John was a man who took what he wanted and one thing he had wanted more than anything else was the throne of England, even though his nephew, Prince Arthur of Brittany had a greater claim to it. Arthur was the son of Geoffrey, John's elder brother who had died in 1186. However, on his deathbed Richard the Lionheart declared John to be his heir and their mother Queen Eleanor of Aquitaine supported her son against her grandson.

But after his coronation John always feared that Arthur would try to usurp him and his nephew did in fact make an attempt to try and win the support of the French territories. For this Arthur was imprisoned by John's men in the castle at Rouen where he mysteriously disappeared and was never seen again. Rumours abounded, but although John was accused of having him murdered, nothing was ever proved.

But John's reign was still not secure. Arthur had a sister, Princess Eleanor, and although at the time the English people would not readily have accepted a woman on the throne she was still a threat to the King, for if she were to have a son, that child would also have a prior claim to the throne. To make sure that this never happened the princess was brought over from France by her Uncle John and 'kept' in his castle at Bristol. After crossing the moat and entering the great gates the unfortunate princess was never to leave the castle. She was closely confined within the keep for a total of 40 years, guarded day and night by four trusty knights lest she should have an opportunity of engaging in a clandestine marriage and producing an heir. It is difficult to imagine what her life must have been like imprisoned within those mighty walls for all those years – and this in the glorious Age of Chivalry.

However, the inhabitants of Bristol did not forget the ill-fated Princess Eleanor; after all she was a hereditary heiress to the crown of England. So the King considered it prudent for the Governor of the Castle to show his royal 'guest' to the public every year to prevent any suspicion of foul play, for after the disappearance of her brother her captivity must have caused some public concern. Each year for the next 40 years Eleanor was allowed to walk around the battlements to be exhibited before the people of Bristol.

When the Barons rebelled against King John and forced him to sign the Magna Carta, Bristol was one of the few places that remained loyal to him. It was from the safety of his great castle in 1216 that he left on that fateful march which would ultimately take him to his death in the Wash.

Eleanor outlived her Uncle John by 24 years. But despite that his son and successor Henry III showed no mercy whatsoever to his cousin imprisoned in Bristol Castle, for even in middle age she was still considered a threat to the throne. After a life spent largely in captivity Eleanor finally died in 1241. At last she was free of the great stone walls of King John's castle.

All
for Love

AS the early morning coach rattled along the rough road out of Bath one day in 1772, one of its passengers must have been feeling very apprehensive. She was 17 years old and, to escape from a disapproving father, was eloping with the reckless but handsome young man who had swept her off her feet. This young man was later to become one of Britain's greatest playwrights; his name was Richard Brinsley Sheridan.

Elizabeth Linley was a beautiful girl who was loved and admired by all. Her father, Thomas, was a musician and employed as Director of Music in the Assembly Rooms. Discovering that his daughter had a good voice and showed a marked talent for music, he trained her as a singer and she regularly gave concerts in the city. There is no doubt that Linley exploited his popular daughter to his own advantage but what shocked Bath society in the year 1771 was his choice of a husband for her, a man called Walter Long. He was 60 years old, she was just 16! The reason was patently obvious, the chosen fiancé being a gentleman of property with an income estimated at £10,000 a year. At first Elizabeth dutifully obeyed her father but eventually could bear the prospect

55

no longer and asked Long to release her from the engagement, which, to his credit, he did.

Richard Sheridan had come to Bath to join his father, who as well as being a professor of elocution was also an actor-manager and had strong connections with the theatre. Young Sheridan was soon caught up in the social whirl of 18th century Bath and when he met Elizabeth Linley he fell head over heels in love with her.

After the severance of her engagement to Long, Elizabeth was escorted by several different gentlemen of means including a family friend called Captain Thomas Matthews. She was captivated by the charming young Sheridan but unfortunately, being poor, he did not stand much of a chance of being accepted by her father as a suitor. The couple must have met furtively on many occasions until at last they could bear the situation no longer. They caught the early coach and together ran as far away from Bath as they could – to France.

Thomas Linley was devastated when he discovered his daughter's elopement and insisted that she had been taken to her ruin. It was rumoured that the runaway couple went through a form of marriage in France, but even if this were true it would have been invalid as they were both under age. When challenged with ruining the girl, Sheridan claimed that he had taken Elizabeth away to rescue her from the unwelcome attentions of Captain Matthews who was a married man. Matthews vehemently denied the charge and there was no evidence that it was true; he was merely a friend of the family. Outraged at the accusation, the Captain inserted a notice in the *Bath Chronicle* of the time calling Sheridan 'a liar and treacherous scoundrel'. The Pump Room gossips revelled in such a scandal.

To try to repair her reputation Sheridan lodged Elizabeth with the nuns in a convent at Lille in northern France and it was here that Mr Linley found her and brought her back to Bath. But public attentions to the girl were so disagreeable that she was soon packed off and sent to live with her Aunt Isabella in Wells.

As a result of his insults and accusations Sheridan was to fight two duels with Captain Matthews. The first time they met in London, Sheridan won, and received an apology – the second duel was to be a much bloodier affair. Richard Sheridan brazenly returned to Bath where the scandal of the elopement was still simmering. Matthews was infuriated by his arrogance and challenged him to the further duel which took place at Kingsdown outside the city. The two men attacked each other furiously with swords, hacking out with the weapons as they rolled together on the ground. Such an event, of course, attracted many spectators and it ended with Matthews stabbing Sheridan with a broken sword. His honour was at last satisfied.

Elizabeth was appalled when she learnt of the duel. She had always insisted on calling Sheridan her 'husband' and, when she heard that he had been wounded, rushed to his side in Bath. The two became inseparable and when Sheridan wrote to Mr Linley pleading for his daughter's hand, he reluctantly consented. What else could he do?

On 13 April 1773 Sheridan finally married his Elizabeth. In the register they are described as bachelor and spinster. Finding himself short of money in his new status, Sheridan tried his hand at writing and had a great success with his first play *The Rivals*, based on the Bath social scene of which he had such intimate knowledge!

Many more successes were to follow and he and Elizabeth moved into a new world in the theatre. But tragedy struck when Elizabeth died at the Hotwells Spa at the early age of 38. Sheridan was stricken with grief and moved permanently to London where he found fame, fortune and even more notoriety.

Mantrap!

EIGHTEEN-FIFTEEN was a bad year for West Country farmers. The spring was cold and the summer wet and miserable resulting in the complete failure of many crops. Food prices soared in the local markets and some poor families who relied on growing their own vegetables in little cottage plots grew weak and neared starvation. The rich local landowners, who were able to buy in supplies from further afield, often appeared unsympathetic to their smaller neighbours and this naturally caused some resentment. To provide their families with food more and more of the poor yeoman farmers took to poaching on the large estates, not in a big way but just occasionally catching a rabbit or bird to help eke out the little food they had.

Poaching had always been practised among country folk. Over the years there was hardly a farmhouse in England which at some time did not contain an illegally caught salmon or brace of birds. Although hazardous it was considered a risk worth taking. However, many poachers were professionals and some London markets relied on regular supplies from such people. As poachers such as these began to use guns the penalties became more severe. An Act of Parliament passed in 1803 made poachers liable to hanging if they were caught armed and resisted arrest. Even these severe measures did not seem to deter very many though. A survey at this time revealed that one seventh of all convicted prisoners had been found guilty of the crime of poaching. So serious did the situation seem to some landowners that they took matters into their own hands and to catch the offenders devised and set cruel 'mantraps'. These consisted of holes with spikes, leg breakers or spring guns which could maim or kill whoever was caught in them.

By 1815 mantraps had officially been banned, but as that inauspicious year progressed gamekeepers in the lower Severn Valley began to notice an increase in poaching on their land. Some, who were aware of the problems of the poorer folk, turned a blind eye to it; after all the odd rabbit would not be missed. But the gamekeepers on an estate at Tortworth in Northavon decided to teach the poachers a lesson. Although they knew the practice to be illegal, they set up a deadly mantrap consisting of a trip wire connected to a loaded blunderbuss gun.

One particular night an unsuspecting local farmer called Thomas Till ventured into Harris's Wood in the hope of catching something for his supper. Local poachers who knew their way around very often set their own traps in remote parts of the woods. That night the man was pleased to find a rabbit in his trap; his family would at least have one good meal that week. No doubt eager to get back home with his catch Thomas Till was not so vigilant as he might have been, for he had the misfortune to fall into the trap – the mantrap – and his head was blown off by the blunderbuss!

Knowing the killing device to be unlawful, Till's family and the local smallholders made sure that his case was brought to court. However, despite the resulting publicity in their favour, the tenants of the Tortworth estate feared for their livelihoods and would not stand up and accuse their powerful landlord, so a non-committal verdict was returned.

The farmers were incensed as they felt that justice had not been done. In an angry mood they met at the house of Farmer John Allen and decided to go into the estate and confront the gamekeepers. They wanted to show their feelings about the dreadful death of their colleague and to explain their position in those dire times. John Allen willingly became their spokesman. They were not violent men and before setting off they agreed that if the keepers did threaten them they would fight like men, with their fists, and not use their guns, for surely the keepers would not dare to kill another of them so soon after the Till case.

So Allen and his party walked boldly into the Tortworth estate. Starving men are determined men, but although tempers ran high they walked in trepidation of what might happen. Predictably the keepers were waiting for them. As they approached, under the tension of the moment a nervous finger must have touched a trigger, for one of the farmers' guns went off accidentally. The situation had reached flashpoint. The others thought this was a signal and started firing haphazardly as they made a frantic retreat. In the chaos that followed one gamekeeper was killed and several others were wounded.

The farmers were all arrested and at the consequent trial the chief gamekeeper swore on oath that he had overheard one of the men say, 'Now Tom Till's debt is paid.' On hearing this the jury believed that it was a raid specifically planned to revenge Thomas Till and that they had intended to take a life for a life. The unanimous verdict was 'Guilty'. John Allen was hanged and the others were transported for life.

Devilish
Deeds

IT is said that the Devil's work is never done; he has certainly been busy in Avon!

In the south of the county, at Banwell, people have been puzzled for centuries by a mysterious 'cross' of turf which is built into the hill. This stands two feet high and is over 70 feet long. One theory is that it might have had some connection with an old system of surveying, perhaps dating back to Roman times. A more popular belief is that long ago the people of the village tried to build an upright cross but each time they raised it the Devil sent a terrific wind and blew it down. In desperation, after this had happened several times they created the grass cross flat on the hillside and so thwarted the Devil for all time.

On the slopes of Worle Hill near Weston-super-Mare is the village of Kewstoke. It was here on the hill that Saint Kew is reputed to have built his hermitage. No trace of the building now remains as it was swept away during a stormy period in the 16th century but a strange tale is preserved in the barbed arrowheads seen incised on stones in the area and in the symbolic carvings on the medieval pulpit in the church.

It seems that when Saint Kew built his cell on the top

of Worle Hill he also made a flight of steps down to the
local church near the coast. These old steps, called 'The
Monk's Steps', still survive.

Kew was known to be a strong man and although he
lived for more than his allotted three score years and ten
his beard is said to have remained as black as coal. One
stormy night a stranger knocked on his door saying that
he had travelled far and lost his way in the tempest. Kew
invited him in and offered him a frugal meal. When he
asked his guest to remove his black hat and gloves the
man refused, drawing his cloak more tightly round himself. As Kew started to say Grace before the meal the
stranger struck the lamp from the ceiling with a mighty
blow. Just before it landed Kew saw that his guest had
cloven hoofs! He now knew the identity of his adversary,
but being a strong man who knew no fear he attacked the
Devil and a terrible fight took place. It ended with Saint
Kew hanging onto the Devil's tail and refusing to let go.
The Devil realised that he had met his match and
vanished in a cloud of smoke – but left his tail behind!

The following morning the local people noticed a
scorched track running through the woods to the hermitage. They feared the worst but when the church bell
began to ring for matins Saint Kew appeared, safe and
sound, at the top of his steps with the Devil's tail in his
hands. Triumphantly he nailed it to the church door –
hence the barbed arrowheads.

The Devil did score one point in this contest though.
After his ignominious defeat he revenged himself by
carrying off one of Kew's steps and casting a spell over
the rest so that each time a step was renewed another
would be missed elsewhere. It is a time-honoured fact
that the number of steps can never be counted by two

persons alike. Any two people visiting Kewstoke today may verify this.

Most of the time, however, the Devil was more successful in his endeavours to tempt the souls of men.

Near the river Chew at Stanton Drew is one of the county's most remarkable antiquities, a group of megalithic stones known as The Devil's Wedding Party. Local legend tells how one Saturday a young couple were married and their union was so popular that the revelries went on long into the night. But when midnight struck, the piper, who was a devout fellow, refused to play any more as it was now the Sabbath. The bride, who was obviously enjoying herself, wanted to keep the party going and swore that she would find another piper to play for them, even if she had to go to Hell to find him.

At that moment strange haunting music was heard. Louder and louder it became, music so exhilarating that the guests just could not stop themselves dancing. The faster the music, the faster they danced, swishing and swirling, round and round. For the piper who appeared, though dressed as an old man, was none other than the Devil himself. Throughout the night they danced on, until exhausted they died one by one. Not only did they die, but were turned to stone! When morning broke, the demon musician returned to Hell, and the wedding party remained, petrified in a circle. They stand today, the place full of an indefinable sense of mystery and stillness.

To the north of the Stanton Drew stones, just off the Chew Magna road, is a vast boulder, though now much smaller than it was originally as it has been hewn and used as road mending material. This stone is known as Hauteville's Quoit. Sir John Hauteville was a well-known Crusader and lived at Norton during the 13th century. He seems to have been a giant of a man and various feats of strength are attributed to him. Once he caught three sheep stealers and carried them, one under each arm and the third in his teeth, up to the top of Norton church tower and threatened to throw them over if they did not mend their ways.

The Quoit is the result of a match of strength between Hauteville and the Devil. Sir John threw the great boulder from the top of Maes Knoll and it landed in its present spot. The poor old Devil must have gone away with his tail between his legs that time, for his throw was all of 'three furlongs' shorter than that of the giant Crusader!

The Devil was always on the lookout for likely victims to populate his underworld kingdom and one such was an old woman who lived alone in a cave near Radstock. Nancy Camel was thought of locally as a godless old miser. She was a stocking knitter by trade and worked ceaselessly day and night to add a few more coins to her ever increasing hoard. When it was known that she even worked on a Sunday the people whispered and would only look at her sideways, believing her to be a witch.

Such a person was an easy catch for the Prince of Darkness and he visited her in her cave one night, tempting her with a sack of gold. This he promised to give her in exchange for her soul which he would claim in seven years time. Greedily eyeing the gold, Nancy agreed, for now she really would be rich. But even with the Devil's bullion she still continued to knit stockings in order to scrape together even more money. People dared not refuse to buy her produce in case she cast a spell on them!

When the seven years were nearly up the old woman's

conscience began to prickle and she became frightened, wondering what might happen to her. Meekly she went to a priest and confessed her sins. The good priest promised the miser forgiveness if she would throw away the Devil's gold and turn to God. She agreed. But when she returned to her cave she found it was just not possible. The lure of the gold was too strong. She went back to the priest and told him a lie, pretending that she had thrown the gold down a deep well.

Seven years to the day after the Devil's visit a fearful storm occurred and above the howling of the wind the local folk heard the rattle of wheels and the crack of a great whip. Then a terrible scream rang out from the cave. The following morning the priest and a few brave villagers went to seek Nancy, but she had gone. Deep marks of wheels and hoofs on the rock of the cave and the sickly smell of sulphur proved the identity of who it was that had carried her off. No one ever attempted to find the gold!

Nancy Camel was not the only one in the area to sell her soul but when a similar offer was made to Sir Hugo de Sturden, he managed to cheat the Devil of his due.

In the wall of the north aisle of Winterbourne church is the effigy of a knight who is popularly believed to be Hugo de Sturden. He is reputed to have been a rogue and at one time was outlawed for 'unsavoury deeds'. Rumour has it that he sold himself to the Devil in return for certain favours, agreeing at the time that when he died he would not be carried into the church with either his head or feet forward; nor would he be buried in the churchyard.

After his life of evil, however, Sir Hugo repented and received holy communion almost at the point of death.

To cheat the Devil still further he instructed that his coffin be carried into the church sideways and that he should be buried in the church wall.

Thwarted once again, on his way back to his lair, the Devil no doubt stopped off near Wrington for a doleful wake with his comrades in Goblin Combe!

Princess Caraboo
of
Javassu

❧

ONE spring evening in 1817 the villagers of Almonds-bury were surprised to see a stranger wandering through their village. Now strangers were not that un-common in the village, being close to the city of Bristol and near the river Severn, but this one had what was termed 'an interesting appearance'. She was a dark, attractive young woman, with long black hair, wearing a brightly-coloured Eastern-style dress and on her head a jewelled turban complete with feathers!

The villagers watched curiously as she walked up to one of the cottages and knocked on the door. When the cottager opened the door, to his amazement the woman uttered some strange words. He was dumbfounded. Then, when she used sign language, pointing to her mouth and folding her hands against her cheek, he realised she was asking for food and shelter.

The poor man did not know quite what to do. In those days villages were responsible for the well-being of their own poor and nobody wanted to assist an outsider because this would increase their poor rates. The other villagers must have advised the man to take the stranger to Knole Park House up the road, where the Squire, Samuel Worrall, was a well-travelled man. Squire Worrall would know what to do.

As the locals anticipated, the Worralls took pity on the bizarre young woman and invited her into their house; but they too were baffled by her strange behaviour. The girl kept repeating the word 'Caraboo' and pointing at herself. Mrs Worrall assumed this was her name, and from her richly embroidered dress, jewels and gold earrings also assumed she was from a royal Eastern family. They decided to call her Princess Caraboo.

Next day the local parson, hearing about the strange girl, called at Knole House bringing with him several books with illustrations. He thought she might recognise some of the pictures and he would thus be able to establish her identity. As he flipped through the pages, Caraboo remained dumb most of the time, until he showed her a picture of a boat sailing along the coast of an Eastern land, at which the girl grew excited and touching the picture repeated the word 'Javassu, Javassu'. If the girl had indeed come from the East Indies, how she came to be wandering alone in a West Country village was certainly a puzzle. The parson and the Worralls must have deliberated long and hard on the subject. They eventually came to the conclusion that she must have been kidnapped or sold into slavery (a common practice at that time) and somehow managed to escape.

Whilst staying with the Squire and his family at Knole Park House, Caraboo settled down into a strange routine. Of all the drinks offered to her she would only drink tea, which was then considered an upper-class luxury. She shunned any dish containing meat and would only eat vegetables. Mrs Worrall watched with interest as her guest said prayers to what sounded like 'Allah Tallah' and prattled excitedly before scenes of Eastern life which appeared in the decoration at Knole House. The girl performed exotic dances to the delight of the Worralls' guests and even showed skill in the martial arts. Samuel Worrall, himself a trained swordsman, failed to disarm her in a combat with single sticks.

Princess Caraboo, who insisted on wearing her turban and exotic clothes in public, was now introduced by the Worralls into Bristol society. The mysterious princess caused a sensation, was invited to parties in several of the big houses and soon became a popular celebrity. She had her portrait painted and notices appeared about her regularly in the local press. It seemed that everyone wanted to meet the Princess Caraboo – particularly a Mrs Neale.

Mrs Neale had become curious about the Princess after reading about her in the local newspaper and on hearing her neighbours' gossip, so made a point of going to see Caraboo when she paid a well-publicised visit to the Pump Room in Bath. When she had had a good look at her Mrs Neale's suspicions were confirmed; she immediately wrote a letter to Mrs Worrall at Knole Park. What she wrote left Mrs Worrall thunderstruck. This 'Princess Caraboo', she wrote, was without doubt her runaway servant girl, Mary.

Horror and consternation reigned. The Princess was brought before Mrs Neale and when confronted by that lady, Caraboo broke down. She was, in fact, Mary Wilcox, who, after being beaten persistently by her father, had run away and got a job as a servant. After she had run away for a second time Mary had at first gone to London where she survived by begging. Eventually she had left London and wandered the country with a band of gypsies.

During her wanderings with the gypsies she had met and married someone she described as an 'Eastern Gentleman' called Baker Stendht. It was he who had given her the clothes and jewels, taught her to dance and instructed her in the martial arts; possibly with the idea of them joining a group of travelling performers, or a circus. That was not for Mary and she had run away from him, too!

Mrs Worrall was horrified. But after scolding her 'princess' for the deception, she softened, and refrained from punishing her. Mary, she concluded, had to live by her wits to survive. However, this latest deception was a scandal upon society of humiliating proportions, and for Mrs Worrall it meant that Mary could no longer stay in the Bristol area. The best thing, she decided, was to send her to America to start a new life; so Mrs Worrall bought Mary a passage to Philadelphia where there were plenty of rich families offering domestic jobs to English girls. And that was the end of the brief but rather splendid reign of Princess Caraboo of Javassu!

The
Duking Days
at Keynsham

KEYNSHAM, built at a point where the river Chew joins the river Avon, must have witnessed many events throughout its long history, but perhaps the most renowned took place on 25th June 1685.

Nowadays a huge chocolate factory dominates the quiet river meadow known as Sydenham Mead. It was here just over 300 years ago that a ragged, quixotic army set up camp after a long, optimistic march. The army was poised to capture the city of Bristol the following day. If it had been successful the course of history in this country might have been different. As it was the final result of that campaign was to be the bloody carnage of the Battle of Sedgemoor.

King Charles II and his Queen, Catherine of Braganza, had no children. Queen Catherine had even visited the healing springs of Bath to try and effect a cure for her barrenness but without success. So when Charles died in February 1685 it was his brother James II who succeeded him. There was, however, another contender for the throne and that was Charles' illegitimate son, James,

Duke of Monmouth. The beloved 'Protestant Duke' was trained as a soldier and respected for his courage and military bearing. In the end however his illegitimacy was too great a barrier for a prospective King of England and his uncle, although a Roman Catholic, was declared the rightful heir.

Despite this churchmen and people alike were suspicious of a Catholic monarch and so strong was public opinion that the Duke of Monmouth was encouraged to try to make himself King in the name of Protestantism. He was in Holland when his father died and the only way he could enter the country and claim the crown for himself was by armed invasion. With the help of supporters in Protestant Holland he managed to equip a small fleet and set sail for a port in the south west of England. He chose the West Country for his landfall because he felt he would gather support there from fellow Protestants, especially those who remembered him from a State Tour he had made in 1680.

Within days of his landing on the Dorset coast at Lyme Regis in June 1685, perhaps as many as 6000 enthusiastic West Countrymen had rallied to his cause. The response was very encouraging. This period of loyalty to the Duke of Monmouth became known as 'The Duking Days'.

The rebel army was composed mainly of peasants and small farmers who, though high in spirits, had received no military training and were poorly disciplined and badly armed. They carried axes, pitchforks or even clubs. One group was equipped only with scythes, but when attached securely to eight ft. poles, the blades produced a deadly weapon. The troop of 'scythemen' was about 500 strong and was greatly feared. The lack of proper weapons was made up for by the bravery and determination of the men to fight for a Protestant king.

Men from the smallest of villages left their homes to go 'a Duking' and as the ragged army swelled to 10,000 and resolutely pressed on they gave the impression that the objective was to take London. However, their leader, himself an experienced soldier, and his military advisers had other ideas. Before attempting to capture the capital, he must first take Bristol, a city of immense strategic importance. It was known to be strongly Protestant and through its great port reinforcements and supplies would readily be available. If Monmouth could hold Bristol and the West Country, the Protestant land-owning gentry throughout the land might be encouraged to join in the rebellion and depose James.

The King had been kept informed of his nephew's movements and when it was realised that he was not heading straight for London sent out a strong force of trained soldiers to defend Bristol. Many of the city's leading Protestant churchmen were imprisoned so that they could not help the approaching rebels.

The Duke's intelligence agents had advised him that the south of the city was very strongly fortified, so the best way to attack would be from the east through the cover of the Kingswood forest. This meant crossing the river Avon – and the only convenient bridging point on their route was Keynsham.

At the start of the campaign when spirits were high the weather had been fine, but as they progressed through Somerset the skies darkened and for days it poured with heavy rain. The 'Pitchfork Army' had to march along roads ankle deep in mud, their tattered clothes sodden and, as their shoes wore out or fell to pieces, many walked barefoot. When exhausted and footsore they eventually reached Keynsham, they found to their dismay that the bridge had been destroyed by King James' men.

There were only three bridges across the lower Avon in those days, the other two being at Bristol and Bath. Although it meant losing time, in desperation Monmouth ordered his men to repair the Keynsham bridge as best they could. So early on the morning of 25th June the zealous army finally crossed the Avon and assembled on Sydenham Mead. It was at this point that the Duke of Monmouth made his biggest strategic mistake.

As his army had been marching for weeks and were wet, tired and hungry, he took pity on them and decided to camp for the night on the Mead instead of advancing immediately and attacking Bristol. This further delay gave the King's men an advantage. They now had time to muster and during the night the cavalry made a vicious attack on the camp in Keynsham meadow. Discipline was slack and look-outs had not been posted. The rebels were taken by complete surprise and panicked. As they fled in all directions, many were killed. Luckily it was a quick raid and the Duke managed to escape.

This attack at Keynsham, although a relatively small affair, marked the beginning of the end of his campaign for the Crown. Realising the enormity of the task, his nerve began to fail him and he now made his second mistake. He abandoned the idea of taking Bristol, as James' soldiers were obviously in command there, and marched instead in rain and darkness along the south bank of the Avon towards Bath where he believed he had many supporters. Surely the people of Bath would welcome him?

Even if the Duke had taken Bath it would have been a

disaster, for he and his army could easily have been besieged in the town. Furthermore, since James' coronation the city of Bath had become a royal stronghold and when the citizens heard that a rebel army was approaching they locked the city gates. Later, when Monmouth's messenger approached the city gates, holding a flag of truce, and summoned the citizens to surrender – they shot him!

After the wretched Keynsham incident and dismayed by the hostile attitude of Bath, many of the rebels deserted. They were mostly simple men whose farms and families had suffered during their absence, and it was now the hay-making season; some of them, perhaps with a sense of foreboding, straggled furtively home. Morale among those remaining was at a low ebb and Monmouth's own position was pretty desperate. He thought of getting help from the West of England woollen towns but after yet another defeat at Norton St Philip he decided to retreat. So with what was left of his followers, now believed to number only about 3,000, he headed south, closely pursued by the King's militia.

For those who remained loyal 'The Duking Days' ended on 6th July 1685 with the Battle of Sedgemoor, which was to be the last battle fought on English soil. The brutal slaughter at that battle and its bloody aftermath under the infamous Judge Jeffreys still haunts the memory of the West Country. Who could forget the makeshift gallows constructed in every small town and village and the rotting corpses swaying from them; corpses which had been specially treated with salt and tar to make decomposition a slow process. The luckier ones, if they could be so described, about 800 in number, were transported as slaves to plantations in the West Indies.

Monmouth himself fled from the battlefield a broken

man, only to be hunted down several days later and captured. He did not claim any mercy from his uncle nor did he receive any. He was duly sentenced to death and on 15th July 1685 was beheaded. As a final humiliation it is said that it took the executioner, Jack Ketch, five chops of the axe before the handsome head of James, Duke of Monmouth was finally separated from his body.

The Phantom
of
Brockley Combe

BROCKLEY COMBE, in the Woodspring district of Avon, is an enchanting wooded valley and a favourite beauty spot for local people. Brockley Wood now boasts a Nature Trail and during the day when the sun is twinkling through the leaves of the tall trees it is difficult to imagine a more delightful place. But as dusk falls, visitors are glad to leave the Combe. This primitive woodland takes on a totally different character at night and, it is believed, harbours a ghost.

At the beginning of this century at a country inn near Brockley, the landlord was entertaining his customers with a story about a group of gypsies. It seems that they had been spending the night in the Combe when they had heard the sound of a heavy vehicle coming along the track at a great speed. Coming towards them they saw a black coach, or hearse, drawn by four black horses. As the coach drew near they saw to their astonishment that the driver had no head! Terrified, the gypsies had fled from the Combe and had not returned there since.

As the landlord ended his tale, amid the 'oohs' and

'aahs' of the listeners, one man scoffed. 'Ghosts', he declared, 'there ain't no such thing', and just to show his contempt for the story let it be known that when he left the inn that night he would walk home through the Combe. When the time came and the man took his leave, the other regulars looked at one another knowingly.

In the dead of night Brockley Combe is a silent obscure place where the trees and rocks can take on weird forms in the moonlight. After the warmth and cheer of the inn, the man felt a little uneasy as he made his way along the dark track and began to wish that he had taken the main road home. Suddenly he heard coming towards him the sound of heavy wheels, hoof beats and strange voices. The man trembled and picked up a stone, reassuring himself all the time that ghosts were merely a figment of the imagination. From around the corner a vehicle appeared and instinctively the man threw the stone with all his might. The vehicle came violently to a halt. Just then the moon came out fully and he saw, to his amazement, that he had thrown a stone at a wagon containing the local football team, who were taking a short cut through the Combe on their way back from a victory celebration in a nearby village! The revellers shouted angrily at the man, for the stone had just missed hitting their driver. Full of high spirits – and cider – the lads decided to teach him a lesson. They jumped out of their wagon and started to chase him through the Combe.

He had hardly begun to run with the young men hard on his heels when, without warning, out of the darkness there appeared a huge, black hearse drawn by four snorting horses! This time it really was the phantom coach. They all witnessed it and froze with fear as it and its headless driver passed by.

Then it was gone. Silence returned. The football team raced back to their wagon and the driver set off at a cracking pace. As for the man from the inn, he ran home as fast as his legs would carry him without stopping for breath. For a week after the incident he was a nervous wreck and during the rest of his lifetime he never again ventured into Brockley Combe.

Brunel:
Great Western
Genius

DURING the 19th century Bristol was privileged to
have working in its midst the great engineer Isambard Kingdom Brunel, the prodigious son of Frenchman
Marc Brunel and Sophia Kingdom. He was the tech-
nological genius of his day. Born in 1806, Brunel was a
precocious infant who by the age of six had already
mastered the principles of geometry. Marc Brunel, an
engineer himself, recognised his son's potential and sent
him first to a good English boarding school and then, at
the age of 14, to Paris to study mathematics. At the end
of his studies Isambard returned to London and worked
for his father on a project to build a tunnel under the
Thames.

On several occasions in his life Isambard Brunel had
narrow escapes from death. The first of these occurred in
May 1827. He was working in the Thames tunnel when
the roof collapsed. The tunnel flooded and Brunel and
the other workers were fortunate to escape with their
lives. The following January it flooded again. This time
young Brunel was knocked senseless in the swirling

waters but his body was borne along by a tidal wave and thrust up one of the shafts; thus he was luckily saved once more and suffered no more than a broken leg. Work on the tunnel was suspended.

During his convalescence from the second accident he amused himself by entering a competition to design a bridge to span the Avon Gorge at Clifton in Bristol. His bold, novel idea for a suspension bridge with Egyptian-style ornamentation impressed the judges and was chosen as the winner. Bristol beckoned and in the summer of 1830 he travelled there by coach to build the bridge. Later he was to refer to it, his first design success, as 'my first child'. It certainly suffered from growing pains.

Brunel had a rough introduction to the city of Bristol for 1830 was the year of the Riots when, because of the rejection of the Reform Bill in Parliament, the whole city was in turmoil. As soon as he arrived the young engineer was conscripted as a special constable to help restore law and order. Due to the riots and the consequent damage to the city, work on the suspension bridge was shelved 'temporarily'. It was to be five years before construction was able to begin.

Meanwhile Brunel was employed on engineering work to improve Bristol Docks and it was while he was working there that he came into contact with Thomas Guppy and a group of promoters who were planning to build a railway from London to Bristol. The project excited him and he was appointed Company Surveyor.

Brunel became a 'workaholic'. He spent up to 20 hours a day travelling up and down the proposed route in a black britzka carriage, the inside of which he had designed himself in order to keep his plans and instruments together. It also carried a case containing 50 cigars, to which he was very partial! He even slept in his carriage whenever he had a chance and wherever he happened to be.

The building of the railway was an enormous task. It not only involved marking out the London to Bristol route but also the connections with Cheltenham, Gloucester, Worcester, Oxford, Exeter, Plymouth and South Wales; it would truly live up to its name – the Great Western Railway.

By 1835 with the rail project well in hand, Brunel was still engaged by the Bristol Docks Committee and he was also now supervising the building of his 'first child', the Clifton Suspension Bridge, on which work had just recommenced. In 1836 he somehow managed to find time to meet and marry Mary Horsley and later to produce three children, two boys and a girl. It was while playing with his children that he nearly lost his life for the third time. He enjoyed creating tricks for the young-sters and one day was trying to make a half-sovereign magically appear from his mouth when he accidentally swallowed it. The coin lodged in his throat and started to choke him. A surgeon tried desperately to free it using a two foot long pair of forceps but to no avail. Despite the discomfort, Brunel eventually designed his own salvation consisting of a device which would whirl him head over heels and by which he hoped the coin would emerge by centrifugal force. It did. The great engineer stood up a little dizzy but otherwise unharmed.

The Chief Locomotive Assistant on the GWR was another talented man, Daniel Gooch and he and Brunel, who became lifelong friends, supervised the progression of the railroad together. Despite opposition a 'broad gauge' rail had been adopted which was thought to be most suitable for the flat, straight run from London to Bristol. Brunel also designed the buildings for Paddington and Temple Meads stations. Temple Meads proved a problem, for as its name suggests, it was built on some marshy ground just outside the city. The supports for the building had to be sunk to a great depth in order to give it the necessary stability.

The biggest obstacle the engineers had to deal with was the tunnel through Box Hill between Corsham and Bath. Two miles long and through solid rock, it was to be the longest and most difficult tunnel ever attempted. Working on his father's tunnel under the Thames had given him the expertise and Brunel boldly organised 4,000 men and 300 horses on shift work round the clock. A ton of gunpowder and at least a ton of candles were used each week. A local brickmaker used a hundred horses and carts solely to carry 30,000,000 bricks to the site. Box Tunnel took two and a half years to complete and during its construction more than a hundred men lost their lives.

The Great Western Railway, described at the time as 'the finest work in England' was finally completed in 1841. On the inaugural trip Brunel rode on the locomotive platform and Thomas Guppy, one of the original Bristol backers, is said to have danced on the roof of one of the carriages in sheer delight.

One of the directors of the GWR had once expressed his concern to Brunel on the length of the line. The engineer's reply was typical of him, 'Why not make it longer and have a steamboat connection from Bristol to New York and call that the Great Western?' It was from this remark that Guppy and some other backers founded the Great Western Steamship Company. Engineers of the time, including Marc Brunel, believed that no ship relying solely on steam power could carry enough fuel for an ocean crossing. Brunel's imagination and engineering vision now turned to ship design and he soon realised that bigger ships did not necessarily need more fuel to propel them through the water. His first prototype, the *Great Western*, although outwardly a wooden-built paddle boat, was to be the first true steamship to cross the Atlantic.

Though there was a fire on a trial run of the *Great Western* she did complete the first historic crossing in April 1838 in 15 days with coal to spare (about 200 tons in fact). The steamship age had arrived and America welcomed the genius of the *Great Western*. On her return to Bristol she was met with what the *Bristol Mirror* described as 'flag-flying, bell-ringing general rejoicing.'

With this success behind him Brunel then started on the design of a second vessel. This was yet another completely revolutionary design, built of iron and powered by a screwpropeller instead of paddles. When built, it was an enormous ship. She was named the *Great Britain* and launched by Prince Albert in 1846. It was found to be almost impossible to navigate the gigantic ship out of Bristol's old docks and down the Avon, so that thereafter she sailed from Liverpool. The Great Western Steamship Company had lasted for ten years and during that time only owned two ships. But what great ships they were! Brunel's fine vessels marked the advent of a new era in sea transport throughout the world.

When he returned to London in 1850 Brunel's beloved 'first child', the Clifton Suspension Bridge, had once more been abandoned due to lack of funds and it was still incomplete when, worn out by years of overwork, the great man died, in 1859.

After Brunel's death, a new bridge company was formed, fresh capital was raised, and the bridge was finally opened in December 1864, a lasting memorial to the man who came to the city to build a bridge across the Avon but was eventually to provide, via the city of Bristol, a 'bridge' between London and New York.

A
Sextet of Saints

MANY towns and villages in the county of Avon have saintly connections. According to tradition for instance, the town of Congresbury was founded by Saint Congar, who as a young man had quarrelled with his royal father, the King of Cornwall, and run away from home. One night he had a dream in which he saw a wild boar running, then stopping and lying down to rest in a river meadow near some reeds. Congar travelled north hoping to join a religious community but one day during his journey he came across the very place he had seen in his dream and believed it to have been a vision showing where God wished him to settle. He immediately set about building a church in that river meadow with the only materials then available to him, wattle and daub.

Being an educated young man of royal birth, Congar's piety was well respected and the local country folk soon began to visit his church and consult him on their religious and family problems. Over the years he worked with Saint Petroc and Saint Cadoc in spreading the gospel throughout the locality and was even believed to have worked miracles among the people. One such miracle was that while preaching a sermon one day he stuck his staff in the ground where, to the amazement of all, it immediately took root and sprouted. Today in Congresbury churchyard there is an ancient yew tree affectionately known as 'Saint Congar's Walking Stick'. On hearing of this miracle the Saxon King, Ine, provided funds to build a monastery near the little church and gradually the wattle and daub were replaced with stone and a settlement grew up around it, becoming known as Congarsburgh.

Like many other holy men at that time Saint Congar undertook the long pilgrimage to Jerusalem and it was while he was there that he died. But such was his reputation that his followers brought his body back to be buried in the town which he had established, Congresbury.

To the north of the county at Oldbury-on-Severn the parish church is in a truly splendid position. It is built on a perfect circular mound just outside the village, overlooking the Severn estuary. The mound is almost certainly artificial and was probably a place where pagan religious rites were performed. Later, when the Romans settled in the area, they built a temple to their gods on the same site. No one knows exactly when the first Christian church was erected there; parts of the present church are very old, but its dedication to Saint Arilda must be unique, for Arilda was a local saint.

Long long ago, Arilda, a maiden, lived with her family at Kington near Oldbury. The unfortunate girl had a suitor called Muncius, who was a known tyrant, and although he was rich Arilda could find no love for him. He pestered her incessantly and such was his violent temper that when she would not consent to sleep with him he cut off her head!

At the site of her martyrdom was a well, still known as Saint Arilda's Well, and the stones at the bottom of this well are red – said to have been stained by the saint's blood, although in reality it is merely evidence of iron in the rocks. After her death many miracles were attributed to Arilda and her virtue was never forgotten.

Blaise Hamlet to the north of Bristol takes its name from Saint Blaise who, according to legend, was a physician who suffered martyrdom at the hands of the Romans in AD 316. Despite the fact that Blaise was a Roman citizen, he was converted to Christianity and in order to avoid persecution left his home and career and dwelt for a time as a hermit. However, he was eventually captured and it was during his journey to prison that he performed a miracle.

While passing through a village he witnessed a young mother who was tormented because her child had swallowed a fishbone which had stuck in his throat and could not be moved. The boy was gradually choking to death. Blaise took pity on the woman and laid hands on the boy and blessed him. When the saint removed his hands the bone was instantly dislodged. For this act Saint Blaise became the patron saint of sufferers from sore throats.

The miracle did not apparently impress his Roman captors and poor Blaise was thrown into prison with other Christians to await execution. His martyrdom eventually took the horrific form of having his flesh torn with sharp iron combs, following which he was beheaded. Because the iron combs used in his torture were implements used in the process of woolcombing,

Blaise was also adopted by the woolcombers as their patron saint.

In times long ago sheep would have grazed in the hills around Blaise hamlet so the area was very probably populated by wool workers. Perhaps during the course of their work some of the fluff from the fleeces used to get into their throats and cause irritation, so there would have been a great need among such a community for a chapel dedicated to the patron saint of both woolcombers and sore throats! At one time there was such a chapel on the Blaise Castle estate but sadly this has long since disappeared.

The town of Keynsham in the Avon valley between Bristol and Bath is probably named after Saint Keyne, a 5th century princess. She was the daughter of Brechan, a Welsh prince, who had 24 children, 15 of whom became saints! Keyne, a devout girl and reputedly a great beauty, fled across the river Severn to escape from her many suitors.

After many years of wandering Keyne eventually sailed up the river Avon looking for a quiet place in which to settle and build an abbey. At a spot near a bend in the river, a local chief gave her a plot of land, but he was not being as generous as he had at first appeared – the land was infested with snakes and had no value to anyone else. However, these serpents proved no problem to Saint Keyne who by the power of her purity and prayers turned them all to stone. The ammonite fossils found so abundantly in the Keynsham area today are said to be the remains of the petrified snakes.

Following the clearance of the serpents, Saint Keyne founded her abbey. Under the direction of its pious abbess it prospered. It was here that Keyne died and it was reported that when the earthly spirit left her it was carried to heaven in a blaze of light.

The Romanesque style Catholic church in Oldfield Park, Bath, is dedicated to Saint Alphege who was a Saxon martyr and one time abbot of the city.

Alphege came from a very wealthy family but as a young man relinquished all his riches in order to enter the church. He first became a Benedictine monk at the Abbey of Deerhurst, where, because of his family background, people of rank and wealth came to him for comfort and guidance. When Dunstan of Glastonbury heard about the popularity of the young monk he appointed Alphege to be Abbot of Bath. Later Dunstan rose to become Archbishop of Canterbury and when he died in 1011 it was Alphege of Bath who succeeded him.

Unfortunately, the following year 1012 proved to be a bleak one. As it progressed Danish invaders gradually overran the whole of southern England. People living near the coast were starving and broken in spirit due to the constant pillaging and attack. Alphege bravely preached out against the heathen practices of these invaders and made himself very unpopular with their leader, Jarl Thorkil. King Ethelred (suitably nicknamed 'The Unready') and his army seemed unable to hold back the ravaging Danes and they eventually reached Canterbury. After a siege lasting 20 days Alphege was captured, carried off and held to ransom. He was imprisoned in one of the Danish longships offshore for a total of seven months and the huge sum of 48,000 pounds weight of silver was demanded for his release. The virtuous Alphege sent a message to his people forbidding them to pay such an enormous ransom for his freedom as it would most certainly have impoverished the church.

The Danes knew nothing of this command and continued to wait. Then one night, in a drunken fury, they dragged Alphege from his floating prison and started to stone him. The Norsemen took an evil delight in this cruel and slow torture and when the victim was too weak to stand any longer he sank to his knees and started to pray. On seeing this one of the Danes is said to have gone berserk and picked up the bone of an oxen and split open the saint's skull. The following morning Thorkil was filled with remorse and allowed the Saxons to carry away the broken body of the martyr and bury it. Very shortly after his death Alphege was sanctified and in time the Danes accepted the Christian faith.

There is evidence of a really unusual saint in the church at Chew Stoke, where there is an altar which is dedicated to Saint Wilgefortis. In times gone by it was she who was invoked by women who suffered from troublesome husbands. She was very popular in Tudor times and Sir Thomas More reported cases of women praying to Saint Wilgefortis.

Wilgefortis herself was a devout lady who dedicated her life to the service of God but because she was also very beautiful had great difficulty in trying to avoid men and thus keep her vow of chastity. Even though she became a nun she still received many proposals of marriage and this infuriated her. Wilgefortis prayed hard that she might become unattractive and so discourage these persistent suitors. It seems that her prayers were answered for overnight she grew a beard!

Death
in the
Forest

AS its name suggests Kingswood was at one time part of a very extensive royal hunting forest which stretched from the Mendips to the Severn. When Bristol was merely a small settlement at a bridging point on the Avon, the Saxon kings of Wessex built a palace at Pucklechurch and had a hunting lodge deep in the forest. It was a perfect place in which to get away from the affairs of state and enjoy the thrill of the chase. This 'forest' was not an area consisting solely of dense trees and undergrowth; certainly there were such parts, but it was mainly scrub and open heathland – a terrain ideal for hunting.

In Anglo-Saxon times hunting and falconry were the most popular pastimes of the 'royals'. Huge hunting parties were organised for tracking stag, roebuck, hare and rabbit to provide meat for the table of the king and his retinue. The hunt was also considered excellent training for the warriors as it gave them an opportunity to practise and perfect their skills with the bow, spear and sword. For a more exciting day's sport, they would hunt wolves, foxes and fierce wild boars which roamed in the forest. Falconry too was a favourite sport. The king's falconer, who looked after the birds, was a respected member of the court. The best falcons could provide the larder with plentiful supplies of wildfowl and even herons.

Being constructed of wood, as with most Saxon buildings, nothing now remains of the hunting lodge nor the palace at Pucklechurch. The only evidence we have for its existence is a vague reference on the map, but it was at this palace in the year AD 946 that one of the most tragic episodes in Saxon history occurred, when the king himself met death in the forest.

In that year King Edmund I of Wessex, grandson of Alfred the Great, was staying at the Pucklechurch palace at the time of the Feast of Saint Augustine. This festival was a high spot on the Saxons' calendar, for it was Augustine who had first introduced them to the Christian gospel. That particular year, which was the sixth of his reign, Edmund decided to give a great celebration banquet and invited many guests to his palace in the heart of the forest.

During the course of the evening the feasting was infiltrated by a known robber, called Leolf, whom King Edmund had banished for his villainy many years before. The man, who still bore a grudge against the King, mingled with the guests unrecognised and even helped himself to food and ale from the royal table.

It was the King's steward, Leon, who first noticed the thief and without wanting to draw attention to the intruder approached him quietly, probably with the intention of asking him to leave. His request was met with scorn. Doubtless under the influence of the ale, the surly Leolf attacked the steward and there was a scuffle. King Edmund himself came to Leon's rescue and is said to have seized the robber by the hair and thrown him to the ground. This infuriated Leolf so much that he leapt up and, drawing his dagger, stabbed the King fatally in the breast.

While their royal host fell bleeding to the ground and the killer made his getaway the guests spontaneously cheered and applauded! By now most of them were drunk and they thought the murder was part of a play put on by the King for their entertainment. One can imagine the confusion which followed. Amid the chaos Leolf would have found it easy to melt into the background and make his escape unnoticed. Silence gradually fell in the banqueting hall of the palace as it was realised that the great feast had ended in the ultimate tragedy.

Over the centuries the 'King's Wood' gradually diminished and buildings have sprung up in its place. Siston Common, near Kingswood, is probably all that now remains of the forest where Saxon kings once hunted and where one such king was himself brought to his untimely end.

Revenge
on the
Viking Raiders

THE popular resort of Weston-super-Mare does not have a harbour in the main town but at the south end of the wide sweep of Weston Bay, tucked away in a creek at the mouth of the river Axe, is the small port of Uphill. Uphill was a busy port from Roman times until the beginning of the present century, being one of the few safe anchorages on this part of the coast. The peculiar name for the port, 'Uphill', comes from the Old English 'the place on the pill', a pill in this part of the country being a creek or inlet.

In the 9th century the coast around the Axe estuary was a favourite landing place for Viking and Danish raiders who sometimes made sorties inland. The local people were terrified by these wild, red-haired invaders, who repeatedly destroyed their property and took their livestock. The fishermen and farmers of the Wessex coast were no match for the strength and superior weapons of the Norsemen. Each year as spring approached look-outs were posted on Brean Down and St Nicholas' Hill to watch for the invaders and beacons were lit to warn of any approaching danger.

One particular year the Viking longships were once more sighted making their menacing way up the Channel towards Weston Bay. The warning beacons were lit and panic overcame the people of Uphill. They abandoned their houses, taking with them the few precious possessions which they could carry, and ran to the hills for safety.

At the time one old woman was busy gathering reeds by the sea shore. She too had noticed the beacons but was too old to run, so she hid herself in the rushes and watched while the Vikings tied up their ships and set about their raiding and plundering. After a while she noticed that the tide was beginning to turn; after years of reaping reeds she had learned the fickle ways of the tides in the estuary and knew the very early signs of their turning. Soon the longships began to strain on their ropes. Making sure that no one was in sight, the wise old woman swiftly and silently went from ship to ship cutting the mooring ropes with her sharp reed knife and setting the wooden boats adrift.

The raiders were too involved to notice but the local men in their hiding place soon spotted that the longships were gradually drifting out to sea and they realised that the invaders were stranded. It was a chance not to be missed. They rallied together and using all the weapons they could muster attacked the Vikings, taking them completely by surprise. The slaughter was complete – not one of the Norsemen survived. Their ships were wrecked and the red-haired raiders never again landed in Weston Bay.

Royal Fugitive

AS dusk fell on the battlefield of Worcester on 3rd September 1651 the Royalists knew they were defeated. Cromwell's net closed in, gradually destroying the tattered army, but in the chaos and confusion which followed many managed to escape. Among them was a young man of 21 years who at that moment must have reached the lowest point of his eventful life. With a heavy heart he rode his horse away from the battlefield, sheltered by several of his loyal officers. The young man was Charles II, King of England.

In the days which followed Charles experienced most of the misfortunes which human life can offer – poverty, hunger, weariness and exile. The only course open to him now if he was to avoid the same fate as his father, executed two years before, was to flee the country. His escape plans were frustrated by the fact that a reward of £1,000 had been placed on his head and this must have been a great temptation to some of his poorer followers. He had to be very careful whom he trusted.

While he was lodging in the house of Colonel Lane, one of his most loyal supporters in Warwickshire, it was decided that the King would stand a good chance of escape from Bristol which was at that time the second largest port in the country. A plan was made. Colonel Lane's sister, Jane, had obtained a pass to visit her friend, Mrs Norton, who was pregnant at the time, in Abbot's Leigh, Bristol. Charles was to accompany her.

He took the name William Jackson and, dressed as a servant in sober country grey and a high black hat, dutifully fetched the horse from the stables and waited for his 'mistress' with his hat under his arm. When they were ready to leave, Jane Lane mounted the horse and sat behind her King. As they set off for Bristol she must have been well aware of the consequences for both of them if they were to be caught. She knew that for the next week the life of the King of England was in her hands.

For most of the duration of the Civil War the Parliamentary forces had a stronghold in Bristol, so when Miss Lane and her 'servant' entered Bristol by way of Lawford's Gate, Roundhead troops must have been everywhere. The brave pair courageously rode right through the middle of the city and crossed the river Avon by way of the Rownham Ferry in the Hotwells district. Towards evening they reached Abbot's Leigh and the gabled Elizabethan house which was the home of the Nortons.

As they approached the house they noticed a group of men playing bowls on the lawn. Charles gave a start as he recognised, to his dismay, that a member of the group was one of his former chaplains, a Doctor George. However, playing his part to the full he wrapped his cloak around himself and took the horse to the stables. Meanwhile Jane greeted her friend and asked if she might have a room in the house for her servant as he was unwell and she was worried about him. Mrs Norton instructed her butler, a man called Pope, to make ready a private room with a good fire in which to accommodate the ailing servant.

All went well until at supper Doctor George heard about the sick servant and enquired of Miss Lane about his health. He rather fancied himself as a physician and embarrassed Jane with questions about the man's illness. When he offered to visit the sick man to give his professional advice she must have felt very uneasy. But Charles had by necessity become an excellent actor, for the doctor attended him, took his pulse and advised rest, without suspecting a thing!

Doctor George left the house the following morning. He was gone by the time William Jackson, obviously feeling much better, rose and went to the kitchen for his breakfast. The butler was there along with two or three other men. They ate bread and butter, washed down with ale. During the conversation one of the men started talking about the Battle of Worcester where he had been a trooper in the King's Guards. Trying to allay suspicion Charles asked him to describe the King. The man laughed, 'Not unlike you,' he replied, 'but at least three inches taller!' Upon which William Jackson quickly finished his ale and retreated from the kitchen with his head bowed.

After these two close encounters Charles must have breathed a sigh of relief. But unknown to him at the time, he had been recognised by one member of the household, for when he returned to his chamber later that morning he found Pope, the butler, waiting for him.

When the door was closed the man fell down upon his knees with tears in his eyes and kissed the King's hand, for he was a Royalist and wished to serve his King. This man was to prove a very useful ally. Charles asked him to go down to the harbour in Bristol and try to find a suitable ship to take him to the Continent.

It was to be a very difficult task. That £1,000 reward was too great a temptation and captains and sailors just could not be trusted. Pope had to be very wary with his enquiries; Cromwell's spies were everywhere. After a time he realised that he could not guarantee the King's safety on any of the ships. While in the harbour the old soldier must have been distressed to see merchant ships being used to transport prisoners of war to America, where they would be forced to work as slaves on the plantations, most of them never to return. Some of these unfortunate men were captives from the recent Battle of Worcester.

During the weekend while Pope was valiantly searching for a ship, Charles spent the time in his room quietly resting and feigning illness again. Miss Lane continued to appear anxious about her servant, insisting 'The boy will never recover – he'll ne'er be good again.' One of Mrs Norton's maids, Margaret Rider, developed a romantic passion for the young man and took to waiting on him and making him possets (hot spiced drinks).

With Pope's failure to find a ship to take the King to France it became crucial that he should leave Abbot's Leigh and try another route of escape. Contact was made with Colonel Francis Wyndham, another trusty supporter, who had a house at Trent near Sherborne. He indicated that he would be prepared to help the King from thereon.

All was arranged and Jane was ready to announce her departure to the Nortons when disaster struck. On that very day Mrs Norton had a miscarriage and put poor

Jane in a dilemma, for she could not leave her friend at such a time without a very good reason. Realising the increasing danger to the King if he stayed in Bristol any longer, the ever-reliable Pope saved the situation. He wrote a letter to Miss Lane, supposedly from her brother, announcing the sudden illness of their father. He delivered it to her quite innocently at supper. Jane's reaction did the rest.

The following morning Miss Lane and her faithful 'servant', William Jackson, left the house in Bristol and headed south once more. Exactly a fortnight after the fateful Battle of Worcester, Jane Lane delivered her King into the trustworthy hands of Colonel Wyndham and returned to her native Warwickshire. There were to be many more weeks of furtive travelling and danger before Charles eventually left England for the comparative safety of France.

When he returned to the country in triumph in 1660 King Charles II did not forget his adventures and those who had helped him to escape. To Miss Jane Lane he gave a good pension and an endless shower of presents – including miniatures, jewelled watches, and ornamental snuff boxes. To her brother he made a large grant and to Colonel Francis Wyndham he gave a baronetcy and an annuity of £600 a year.

The
Naughty Nuns
of Barrow Gurney

MONASTIC life flourished in the Middle Ages but while monks were recruited from all classes of society, nuns seemed to have come almost exclusively from the richer families. Convent life was a recognised vocation for women and it seems that the better their family connections the higher they reached in the cloistral hierarchy. It was not unusual to have ex-queens and princesses as heads of medieval abbeys.

To enter a nunnery a girl had to be sixteen years old and able to read and sing. Also, as they were being married to the church, they were required to bring with them a goodly dowry. Compared with the number of monasteries, there were very few nunneries in the country and most were small institutions. Although some had schools and hospitals attached, the hard work was carried out by lay servants while the nuns occupied themselves with more ladylike pursuits of needlework and music. Instead of dormitories most of the sisters enjoyed private sleeping chambers; in fact, they seem to have had all the comforts to which they had been accustomed in their own family life.

The old south aisle of the church of Barrow Gurney was once a nuns' chapel, for nearby stood a Benedictine convent. In the 14th century the Bishops of Bath and Wells had some problems in administering this particular convent, as is revealed by a letter written to the Prioress dated 26th June 1315. In this letter the Bishop of the time threatened her with excommunication if she did not pay more attention to her duties and keep the sisters in order. Apparently, as well as breaking the Rule of Silence, the nuns were leaving the convent at all hours, wearing ordinary dress and jewellery and in some cases even sleeping out!

To try to bring some order to the House this letter instructed the Prioress not to allow her nuns to go beyond the 'vill' and always to walk in pairs. They should possess no other clothing than their habits and never absent themselves from the convent. In the cloisters silence must be observed. Divine Service must be devoutly performed at appropriate times and the Rules should be read aloud daily so that they might be remembered by all. As well as this the Bishop appointed a male administrator, William Sutton, but the sisters made his life such a misery that he resigned voluntarily within a few months. After this the Bishop had no choice but to excommunicate the Prioress of Barrow Abbey.

In her place he appointed Joan de Gurney, who seemed an ideal choice, being a descendant of the founder of the Abbey and a daughter of the noble Gurney family who owned all the land in the area. The family seat of the Gurneys was Richmont Castle at East Harptree. There is no doubt that the Bishop was influenced by his mighty landlords in his recommendation – and that he had obviously not scrutinised Joan de Gurney's appointment too carefully. For it was discovered shortly afterwards that she had not even taken her final vows! This was hastily remedied in a special ceremony and when Joan de Gurney finally prostrated herself before him the Bishop must have breathed a sigh of relief, hoping that would be the end of the matter.

But it was not to be! Prioress Joan turned out to be even more incompetent than her predecessor. She was observed on many occasions visiting friends and relatives, coming and going as she pleased and not even wearing her wimple. She seems to have been treating the Abbey like a private hotel. Obviously she had no control whatsoever over the sisters and discipline went from bad to worse. So after a mere three months in the office, despite her noble connections, Joan became yet another Prioress to be dismissed by the Bishop of Bath and Wells.

The next Prioress was Agnes de Santa Cruce, but the sisters at Barrow were so used to doing just what they pleased that things now got utterly out of hand. So much so that the Bishop wrote a special letter to be read out to the nuns ordering them to behave. But this letter must have been treated with derision, for the sisters carried on with their secular ways. Prioress Agnes somehow managed to hold sway over the wayward nuns for three years . . . but then she died suddenly. Two more prioresses followed but the situation grew no better. By now, for instance, the nuns were not even bothering to attend Divine Service. So, yet another Prioress was appointed.

Matters reached a head when the Bishop received a letter from the Pope enquiring about two of the sisters from Barrow Abbey. Apparently these sisters, Isabella Plyns and Joan Bazen, had quitted Barrow Gurney convent after complaining about the quality of the food and taken themselves off to another convent at Llandaff. They had now written to the Pope asking if they could return to their old quarters at Barrow. Perhaps they had found the food at Llandaff even worse! Upon their return to Barrow Gurney, religious observance and discipline seem to have improved. Perhaps after their experiences in Wales, Isabella Plyns and Joan Bazen made sure that their colleagues realised how very well off they were at Barrow and saw to it that they all respected the new Prioress and conformed to the Rules of the Order. Whatever the reason, no more evidence of disobedience is recorded at Barrow Abbey.

In 1536, along with many others, the Abbey was dissolved during the Reformation and the buildings fell into total decay. Nothing was left to remind the world of the naughty nuns of Barrow Gurney!

The Rip Van Winkle of Timsbury

SAMUEL CHILTON was a strong, seemingly healthy young lad who lived with his mother and worked as a farm labourer in the village of Timsbury in the late 17th century. He was quite normal in appearance being described as having a robust body, not fat, and dark brown hair. But he did have one peculiarity – he used to fall asleep for months at a time!

He could be working, eating a meal or sipping ale at the local inn, when suddenly he would just 'drop off'. When he eventually woke, he would get up and go about his business as usual but he would not speak for about a month afterwards and he never mentioned his strange condition.

The first time it happened he slept from April to August. The only change he noticed in his life was that when he had fallen asleep he was busy sowing barley and oats and when he awoke they were ready to be harvested! Samuel just carried on with his work at the farm as if nothing had happened.

His mother used to worry that he might starve to

death during his lengthy slumbers. Once she tried to force food into his mouth when he was asleep but was unsuccessful as she found his jaws set tight and his teeth clenched, so the poor woman would ensure that she fed him well when he was awake and normal. As she relied on her son for support, Mrs Chilton must have found life difficult while he was sleeping as there would be no money coming into the house.

In time Samuel became quite a local celebrity. When it was known that he had 'dropped off' again the people of Timsbury and the surrounding villages would come to stare at the local Rip Van Winkle. This bothered the lad's mother so much that she decided to call the local doctor to see if anything could be done for him. When he arrived the doctor bled him, taking 14 ounces of blood, then cupped and 'scarrified' him! Nothing he did could rouse the sleeping man.

The story of the Timsbury sleeper spread and soon other doctors came insisting that he must be a fraud. Some of them banged the patient's head against the bedroom wall and stuck pins in him right up to the bone in sensitive parts of his body. Samuel Chilton never felt a thing; he slept through it all without even blinking.

The rarity of the case came to the attention of Doctor William Oliver of Bath, who, intrigued by the matter, travelled on horseback to the Chilton's cottage at Timsbury on 23rd August 1697. He found Samuel's pulse and heartbeat quite regular and his breathing free and easy. Doctor Oliver shook him, shouted in his ear, pinched his nose and mouth for as long as he dared, but all to no avail. Next he tried holding a phial of 'Spirit of Sal Armoniac', which contained quicklime, under Samuel's nose; again there was no response. Despairing, the good doctor poured half an ounce of the spirit up the patient's nose! Still no reaction. Finally he crammed poor Samuel's nostrils with a powder of white Hellebore, the strongest potion he knew, for surely, he thought, no one could be insensitive to that.

Samuel Chilton's nose became inflamed, swelled up and blistered at this indignity. But he never awoke – not, that is, until three months later, on the 19th November!

Mummers
Wassailers
and the
Ashen Faggot

THROUGHOUT the West of England there are many
ancient traditions associated with the Christmas and
New Year period which symbolise that season's eternal
conflict between light and darkness, good and evil. This
tale is about three of them.

Many people enjoying a quiet drink at a country inn
just before Christmas are surprised when in bursts a
group of players dressed in comic and grotesque costumes. They are likely to be mummers. The characters
they portray vary slightly between different areas but
their play is always the same. Good triumphs over evil,
the dead are brought back to life and good cheer is
offered to all. The local performers are quite happy to
dress up in the age-old disguises, for according to tradition no one is supposed to recognise a mummer or it will
break the spell.

The most famous group in Avon are the Marshfield

Mummers. Each Boxing Day in this rather bleak village at the south end of the Cotswolds they act out their play at time-honoured points. They are known as the 'Paper Boys' because their costumes are traditionally covered with narrow strips of newspaper. The first performance takes place outside the church and is preceded by carol singing, introduced perhaps to moderate the obvious paganism of the play! After the collection at the end of each playlet the town crier, ringing his bell, leads the seven mummers in single file through the waiting crowds to the next point.

By late Victorian times, due to lack of interest in folk-lore generally, the Marshfield play had lapsed. It was on the knife-edge of extinction when around the year 1930 the local vicar apparently became aware of his old gardener muttering what sounded like gibberish to himself. On listening carefully, the vicar discovered that it was some form of odd rhyme. He drew the gardener's strange murmurings to the attention of his sister, who was interested in local history, and she recognised that they might be part of an old mumming play. The couple asked the gardener and several other old folk from Marshfield to try hard to remember the play which they had witnessed in their youth and eventually, between them, they re-assembled the entire performance.

So after years of oblivion the custom was revived and has been performed regularly ever since. The seven characters are – Good King William, the evil Beelzebub, Little John, Tenpenny Nit the village idiot, Saucy Jack the sailor, Doctor Phoenix who has the power to raise the dead and the 'modern' character of Father Christmas to offer good cheer as a finale to the entertainment. The

117

parts are played by men from the village, often passing from father to son as the years go by.

Within living memory there were many acres of apple orchards on either side of the river Avon and cider was the local drink. It was in these orchards that the custom of Wassailing the Apple took place on Twelfth Night. The ritual was intended to bring good luck, to protect the trees from evil and to help them bear plentiful fruit in the coming season. The word 'wassail' is derived from the Anglo-Saxon Wes Hál meaning 'be of good health'.

On Wassailing night the farm workers and their families would go into the orchard after dark, taking with them shot-guns and a large pail full of cider. One tree, usually the oldest, was chosen to represent the spirit of the orchard. Ceremonial fires were lighted to start the proceedings, then a great deal of clatter and noise was made in order to awaken the tree spirit. After this the men would encircle the tree and pour the cider around its roots while chanting the rhyme –

Here's to thee, old apple tree,
Whence thou may'st bud and whence thou may'st blow
And whence thou may'st bear apples enow.
Hats full, caps full,
Bushel, bushel sacks full,
And my pockets full too!   Hurray!

At the end of the song shots were fired through the branches to drive away any evil spirits. It was believed that if this ritual were not performed each year there would be no apples the following season.

The 'Ashen Faggot' was the centrepiece of another Christmas tradition. It was a West Country substitute

118

for the yule log. The ash tree had seasonal associations as it was said that Mary lay by a fire made from the wood of the ash at the first Christmas and that the water used to wash the infant Jesus was heated by it.

Instead of a large single yule log the Ashen Faggot was made up of green ash sticks held together with bands of either ash or hazel. It was brought into the house or inn with due ceremony on Christmas Eve. The Faggot was made as large as the hearth would take to ensure that once lit it would burn slowly throughout the 12 days of Christmas.

In country inns with their huge fireplaces, locals would watch the Faggot intently, making predictions from the way the fire burnt as to the time when the bands would break. The breaking of the bands was the signal for a cheery toast. Originally as each band broke the assembled company would demand a free gallon of cider but in later years when the Ashen Faggot made its appearance the landlord provided a free round only with the breaking of either the first or the last band!

Shipshape
and
Bristol Fashion

'Where are we?' I asked.
'Bristol' said Tom.

(Treasure Island)

THROUGHOUT most of its long history Bristol has been a great trading port. Its situation some seven miles from the sea up a highly tidal river may at first seem a disadvantage to a harbour but its distance inland meant that in the early days it was safe from attack by foreign invaders and pirates.

Bristol originated in the 10th century as a Saxon settlement at a convenient bridging point across the Avon. By the Middle Ages 'the place on the bridge' had become a flourishing port by exporting woollen cloth produced in the nearby Cotswolds. It was about this time too, after Henry II married Eleanor of Aquitaine and so acquired many of the finest wine-producing lands of France, that Bristol developed its wine trading connection. Over the centuries it also incorporated wines from Spain and Portugal. When Spanish wines first began to appear on the market, sack, which we now call sherry, became a much sought after drink. It was quoted that '... such is the popularity of this particular Bristolian wine that some will call it Bristol Milk because such wine is the first moisture given to Infants in this city'!

By the start of the 18th century Bristol had become the second biggest maritime port in Great Britain. While London had a monopoly on the East Indian routes, Bristol built up connections with North America and the West Indies and so experienced its period of greatest affluence – its Golden Age.

Although many sailing ships were towed up the river through the Avon Gorge some of the larger ones stayed anchored in the King Road off Avonmouth, their cargoes transported to the docks by barge. At high tide these barges were towed by fleets of rowing boats with sometimes as many as a dozen men in each.

The well known saying 'Shipshape and Bristol Fashion' relates to those great days of sail. As the tides went out each day the anchored ships would ground on the mud of the river bottom and lurch over. Cargoes had to be carefully stowed to fit the shape of the ship in order to avoid damage – therefore 'shipshape'. To withstand this daily battering as they tipped over at low tide the vessels had to be well designed and strongly built – hence 'Bristol fashioned' guaranteed that a ship built in Bristol was stout and seaworthy. With this good reputation the local shipbuilding industry prospered.

While the wine trade with France and Iberia continued, gradually the main trading destination became the West Indies and Virginia. Ships arrived daily carrying sugar, tobacco, rum, cotton, spices and hardwood. But it was in the infamous trade in negro slaves that a few of the Bristol merchants were now making their fortunes.

The system was known as 'blackbirding' and consisted of three separate sea passages. The first passage was from Bristol to West Africa carrying textiles, brass goods, strong drink and firearms. No money changed hands as the goods were bartered with unscrupulous Arab middlemen for slaves. The notorious middle passage was from West Africa to the West Indies. On this voyage the unfortunate Africans were packed into the holds of ships in horrific conditions. Disease was rife and carried off cargo and crew alike. When the ship reached the Caribbean it was not always the end of the journey. Sometimes they had to visit several different islands and mainland America to sell their cargo, depending on demand at the time. The third passage was the return to Bristol. Produce from the West Indies was bought with the proceeds from the sale of the slaves and the ship returned home laden with another valuable cargo.

Despite its unsavoury nature the complete round trip was very lucrative for those prepared to risk it. As crews knew that such voyages were fraught with danger it often proved difficult to man the ships, for as well as equatorial heat and tropical diseases they were also liable to encounter pirates and mutineers. Private pressgangs were common and captains 'bought' crews from local jails; so terrible were prison conditions in Bristol that the men were quite ready to accept the alternative 'to go a blackbirding', whatever the risk.

In the prosperous houses of Brandon Hill and Hotwells the families of these merchants remained ignorant of their activities. Wives knew little about the source of their husbands' wealth and very few slaves were actually brought back to Bristol. The name Blackboy Hill, however, reminds us that it was fashionable at one time to have young negroes as page boys and there is a poignant monument to one such lad in the churchyard at Henbury. His inscription reads:

Here Lieth the Body of
SCIPIO AFRICANUS
Negro Servant to Ye Right
Honourable Charles William
Earl of Suffolk and Bradon
Who died Ye 21 December 1720
Aged 18 years

I who was born a PAGAN and a SLAVE
Now sweetly sleep a CHRISTIAN in my grave

Privateering was another profitable maritime occupation of the 18th century. Privateers were enterprising merchants who were given royal permission by 'Letters of Marque' to attack the commerce of the countries with whom we were then at war, mainly France and Spain. It was a genuine trade. Privateers were not pirates who attacked just anybody; they only attacked enemy ships, bringing anything of worth back to their masters in Bristol. Rich pickings could be had from the Spanish galleons returning from Central America, the Caribbean and even as far afield as Manila in the Pacific.

It was on one of these expeditions, after successfully capturing a Manila galleon, that a privateer from Bristol called Captain Woodes Rogers called at the island of Juan Fernandez to take on water and found the marooned Alexander Selkirk. When his ship returned to Bristol, no doubt with much publicity, it so happened that the writer Daniel Defoe was there, and his subsequent meeting with Selkirk provided the idea for *Robinson Crusoe*.

Defoe was not the only writer to gain inspiration from Bristol. Later, Samuel Taylor Coleridge, who was married to a Bristol woman, is reputed to have written the *Ryme of the Ancient Mariner* after reading an account of Captain Thomas James' voyage from the city to discover the North West Passage. And what must surely be the most famous adventure story of all was the result of a visit to Bristol by Robert Louis Stevenson. Listening to old tales from colourful characters in waterfront taverns stirred his imagination and inspired him to write *Treasure Island*, as this extract reveals:

'Squire Trelawney had taken up residence at an inn far down the docks. Thither we had now to walk, and our way, to my great delight, lay along the quays and beside the great multitude of ships of all sizes and rigs and nations. In one, sailors were singing at their work; in another, there were men aloft, high over my head, hanging to threads that seemed no thicker than a spider's. Though I had lived by the shore all my life. I seemed never to have been near the sea till then. The smell of tar and salt was something new. I saw the most wonderful figureheads, that had all been far over the ocean. I saw, besides, many old sailors, with rings in their ears and whiskers curled in ringlets, and tarry pigtails, and their swaggering, clumsy sea-walk; and if I had seen as many kings or archbishops I could not have been more delighted.'

Today it is difficult to imagine the old 'heart of the city' – what is now that huge roundabout called the

Centre – full of water with tall ships and rigged masts swaying in the breeze. But turn the corner past the statue of Brunel and walk along the cobblestoned King Street towards Welsh Back. In that old street with its 17th century houses, theatre and old inns there still lingers a flavour of Bristol's golden age. And who can possibly walk past the Llandoger Trow Tavern without giving at least a passing thought to Long John Silver and 'Jim lad'.